CW00420882

OVID
Love Songs

ANCIENTS IN ACTION

Also available

Catullus
Amanda Kolson Hurley

Horace
Philip D. Hills

Lucretius
John Godwin

Ovid: Love Songs
Genevieve Liveley

Ovid: Myth and Metamorphosis
Sarah Annes Brown

Spartacus
Theresa Urbainczyk

OVID
Love Songs

Genevieve Liveley

BRISTOL CLASSICAL PRESS

First published in 2005 by
Bristol Classical Press
an imprint of
Gerald Duckworth & Co. Ltd.
90-93 Cowcross Street, London EC1M 6BF
Tel: 020 7490 7300
Fax: 020 7490 0080
inquiries@duckworth-publishers.co.uk
www.ducknet.co.uk

© 2005 by Genevieve Liveley

All rights reserved. No part of this publication
may be reproduced, stored in a retrieval system, or
transmitted, in any form or by any means, electronic,
mechanical, photocopying, recording or otherwise,
without the prior permission of the publisher.

A catalogue record for this book is available
from the British Library

ISBN 1 85399 670 X

Typeset by e-type, Liverpool
Printed and bound in Great Britain by
CPI Bath

Contents

To Sarah

.

Introduction

A woman waits for her husband at the bar of a New York socialite ball. She reaches absent-mindedly for her champagne glass to find that she is holding instead a man's hand. Slowly and deliberately, he drinks champagne from her glass. And he asks her if she has ever read the Latin poet Ovid on the art of love. Sandor Szavost, aging Hungarian roué and Alice Harford's would-be seducer in Stanley Kubrick and Frederic Raphael's film *Eyes Wide Shut*, knows Ovid's *Art of Love* intimately. And when Alice reminds him that Ovid ended his life 'all by himself, crying his eyes out in some place with a very bad climate', he reassures her that the poet had a good time first – 'A very good time.'

Kubrick's Ovid is the playboy poet of popular imagination, notorious for his erotic poetry and his exile from Rome – the love poet who taught Romans how to cheat on their wives and husbands. In fact, this seduction scene from the film *Eyes Wide Shut* might itself have come straight from one of Ovid's own poems. In his *Loves*, Ovid rehearses precisely the same moves as Szavost, as he plans how to seduce a girl at a party – right under the nose of her husband. In his *Heroines' Letters*, he retells one of the best-known love stories of the classical tradition and shows us Paris flirting with Helen in front of her husband Menelaus, taking her wineglass and drinking from the same place that her lips have touched. And in his scandalous *Art of Love*, Ovid recommends this same wineglass technique to all would-be seducers and lovers. Ovid may have ended up all by himself, crying his eyes out in a place with a very bad climate, but the seductive appeal of his poetry has outlived the poet. The emperor Augustus may not have been a fan, but the love poet who became notorious for having a good time is still good for our time.

Should we be surprised by this? Certainly, we might consider how and why Ovid continues to seduce new generations of readers. The question of whether and why ancient poetry appeals to modern tastes has been debated rigorously in recent years and Ovid has figured centrally in considerations of our appreciation of classical poetry generally and Latin love poetry in particular. Critics have noticed that when we think and talk about the past, we can choose to emphasise either its sameness or its difference to our own present. We can highlight the universality of shared 'human' emotions and experiences – particularly those such as love and sex – or we can stress the different social, cultural, and ideological contexts that determine the various historical configurations of these terms. In the case of Roman love poetry, the past is often represented as 'in essence' the same as the present. The men and women who people the world of Latin love poetry are characterised as essentially like us; their feelings, their desires, and their experiences of love and sex are imagined to be fundamentally like our own.

So, it sometimes comes as a surprise to twenty-first century readers to discover that in the same book of love poetry a Roman poet may write of his 'heterosexual' love and desire for a girlfriend, *and* his 'homosexual' love and desire for a boy – reflecting a model of sexuality that is fundamentally different from ours. Ovid casually mentions in his poetry that he prefers women to boys (*Art of Love* 2.683f), but in the opening poem of his *Loves*, he flags the possibility that he might love (and write love poetry about) either sex. He complains to Cupid that he has 'neither a boy nor a girl with long hair' (1.1.19f) to write love poetry about – allowing for the possibility that either would do. In this context, it would be easy to describe Ovid – and his fellow love poets – as 'bisexual'. But the modern term does not quite fit a Roman model of sexuality in which 'heterosexual' and 'homosexual' are meaningless categories of identification and in which sexual orientation is determined not by *who* you choose as a sexual partner but by *how* you choose to have sex with them.

In a similar way, 'love' can be regarded not as a universal and 'historically transcendent' emotion, essentially the same in the first century BC and the twenty-first century AD, but as a cultural construct, varying in different historical contexts. So, although it can seem straightforward enough to translate the Latin term *amor* with the English *love*, this term again doesn't quite fit. English uses the same word to describe our 'love' for our friends, our family, our lovers, and our 'passion' for chocolate – but in Latin, *amor* covers a quite different semantic range. In calling the first collection of his poetry *Amores* or *Loves* (an imperfect translation), Ovid plays with the idea that *amor* or love can have different meanings in different contexts. In Ovid's poetry, *amor* can refer to *Amor* or Cupid (another imperfect translation); to his 'beloved', who is sometimes but not always identifiable as Corinna; to his feelings of erotic or 'romantic' love; to 'sex'; *and* to his book of 'love' poetry. In the opening poem of his *Amores*, Ovid complains that Cupid wants everyone, everything, and everywhere to belong to him (1.1.13-15):

> You have your own realm – and an all too powerful one.
> Why are you claiming new territory, ambitious boy?
> Or is everything everywhere yours?

We might see the same boundless potential in the range of meaning covered by Cupid and *amor*.

In the twenty-first century we still recognise and cherish the Romantic ideal of passionate, sincere, and tender 'love'; a love that seems far removed from the *amor* of the Latin elegists. In this light, some critics have surmised that the Roman poets should bore us because they are 'heartless', 'insincere', and 'insensitive', because they write of love as if it were a game to be played. This argument proposes that an unbridgeable cultural and historical gulf separates us from the Roman poets and their work. An epistemic fault line divides those of us living after the Romantic Age of the late eighteenth and early nineteenth centuries and those living before it. According to this view, we 'moderns' expect poetry about love to be passionate, tender, and sincere: the gamesmanship and stylised insincerity of the 'ancient' Latin love poets is entirely alien to our Romantic sensibilities.

So (it is said), we 'read into' Latin love poetry the sensitivity and sincerity that we want and expect to find there, and in doing so we try to ignore its stylistic devices and literary tropes – its images of love as a kind of slavery or warfare, its extensive use of mythological illustrations. And if these tropes prove too conspicuous to disregard, we try to enjoy their alien qualities instead. Like watching a foreign language film, we try not to let the subtitles impair our enjoyment at the same time as we take pleasure in the 'exoticism' of our experience. So, when we read one of Ovid's love poems and he interrupts the outpouring of his emotion to promise his beloved that his poetry will make her as famous as three mythological heroines – Io, Leda, and Europa – we are conscious that here something strange is happening (*Loves* 1.3.21-4). The mythological allusion reminds us of the literariness of this poem, its artistry and its artifice – and at the same time, it reminds us that we are engaging with something ancient and unfamiliar, foreign and exotic. Whether we disregard it, or whether we register it as an intrusion upon the 'heartfelt' expression of love in the rest of the poem, this device need not distract us from our 'Romantic' reading of this piece as a love poem – although we may wonder at Ovid's choice of three mythological heroines all seduced by the infamous adulterer Jupiter with which to compare his 'one true love'.

Alternatively, we might 'read for' the devices and tropes of Latin love poetry, enjoying its artifice and insincerity, its stratagems and poetics – and giving up the pretence that it has anything 'really' to do with or say about love. So, we can identify and knowingly dismiss the 'pose' of an aristocratic Roman confessing his enslavement to a hard-hearted 'mistress'. We can enjoy the humour in Ovid's use of mythology. When Ovid writes that he is a soldier in Cupid's army (*Loves* 1.9) we can read this as an explicit political statement in which the poet declares his hostility to Augustus and his opposition to Roman militarism. And when he introduces his first collection of love poetry (*Loves* 1.1) claiming that he is not yet actually in love with anyone, we can read this as clear evidence that this love poet is not simply in love with Love or with the idea of love, but with love *poetry*. Such an approach may seem decidedly 'unromantic', yet like the readings of Latin love poetry which look for passion and sincerity, this approach operates with the same clearly defined Romantic ideas of what love and love poetry should and should not be. This too reflects the view that a modern reader requires 'real' love poetry to be passionate, intense, and sincere, and must therefore be alienated by the gamesmanship of Latin love poetry.

But these arguments do not explain Ovid's appeal to a twenty-first-century audience. Like Kubrick's Alice, we can recognise our seducer's stratagems and we can appreciate that he may be playing a game; we can even play too. And, like Alice, we can also find passion, tenderness, and 'romance' in this game. In his *Art of Love*, Ovid warns us of just such a possibility (1.615-18):

But often, the player begins to love for real.
    Often, he becomes what he was at first pretending to be.
So you should be all the more indulgent to those faking it, girls.
    The love that was false once, might become true.

Could it be that Ovid appeals to us because we are now post-Romantics, bored no longer with the artful superficiality of the Romans, but by the trite intensity of the Romantics? It is a nice coincidence that the label 'romantic' is now deemed synonymous with the fanciful and extravagant, the fabulous and fictitious. The myth of Romantic love now seems unrealistic and illusory; the playful 'love' that Ovid writes about seems far more credible. By inverting their positions, we seem to have found that there is no need to find a way across the supposedly unbridgeable epistemic divide between the ancient and modern worlds – we post-Romantics are now on the side of the ancients.

The poetic life of the Roman elegiac lover was dominated by his love for a hard-hearted mistress (*dura puella*) who was beautiful, demanding, and frequently unfaithful. The elegiac lover and poet himself was a lover rather than a fighter, a slave to love rather than a leader of men, and a victim rather than a hero. His poetry celebrated private over public life, love and sex over marriage and children, for here in the looking glass world of elegy, traditional Roman values were inverted: here men were soft (*mollis*) and women were hard (*dura*), and a member of the elite ruling class could be a slave (*servus*) in thrall to his mistress (*domina*). The lyrics of contemporary love songs reflect (although sometimes in a distorted mirror) these same values. Popular love songs of all modern genres – from manufactured boy and girl bands, through hip-hop, rock, soul, indie, folk and country music – celebrate the beauty of a loved one, complain about being 'used', and above all else sing of infidelity and heartbreak. In modern love songs, finding and keeping true love matters more than finding and keeping fame or fortune – although that clearly helps. Falling in love means wanting to have sex with someone – not necessarily wanting to marry them and have children. Love itself hurts, drives you crazy, and leads to bitter conflict. Love is a burning flame, a drug, an addiction, and a disease. Modern love, like its ancient counterpart *amor*, can entail pain, torture, and even 'enslavement'.

But while these parallels between the love songs of the first century BC and twenty-first century AD are striking, we should be wary of assuming that the lover's discourse has therefore remained unchanged over the past two thousand years. The lyrics of modern love songs can represent love and desire using terms that would have been unavailable to the ancient poets. For us 'moderns', love can be like electricity, sex can be like a nuclear reaction, and although Ovid writes about orgasm, as we shall see, he could not have conceived of a multiple orgasm as a 'chain reaction' – as Diana Ross famously sang. Likewise, identifying oneself, as have the band Green Day, as a 'Dominated love slave' in twenty-first-century America is very different from identifying oneself as a *servus* in first-century Rome. And, although we may still understand what it means to have or to be a 'mistress', the full semantic force of the term *domina* has been defused over time. For an aristocratic Roman male like Ovid to declare his servitude to anyone was to be humiliated and degraded, but to declare his enslavement to a woman, to be a 'slave to love', was an explosively charged political and ideological move, designed to be challenging and provocative – and perhaps closer in its rebellious spirit to the Sex Pistols than to Bryan Ferry.

Crucially, contemporary love songs also share their 'insincerity' with Roman love elegy. When Bob Dylan sings 'Corinna Corinna' we don't need to believe that his love song is inspired by or addressed to a real woman named Corinna. When Ovid too sings of his 'Corinna', we need not assume that he is referring to an affair with a 'real' woman; we can accept that 'Corinna' is a convenient fiction. When Tom Waits tells us that 'The piano has been drinking (not me)', we smile. And when Ovid tells us more or less the same – 'my muse has been misbehaving (not me)' – we can also smile (*Sad Songs* 2.353-7):

> Believe me, my character is different from my verse;
>   My life is virtuous, my muse is playful.
> The greater part of my work is fiction and made up,
>   And allows itself more freedom than its own author.
> A book is not proof of character, but honest pleasure.

Ovid writes his first two love songs in the *Loves* before he supposedly meets the woman of his dreams and the object of his desire – prompting disapproval from his 'romantic' readers who regard such cynicism as 'heartless' insincerity. Yet Jarvis Cocker sings in Pulp's love song, 'Something Changed':

> I wrote this song two hours before we met.
> I didn't know your name or what you looked like yet.

And we appreciate the bathos of his heartfelt 'insincerity'. The working title to The Beatles' love song 'Yesterday' was famously 'Scrambled Eggs' – until Paul worked out the tender, moving lyrics that everyone now knows to fit the tune that he had written. For Ovid, too, the metre of his love poetry came first, and the material came second. He begins his *Loves*, in a style better suited to epic than elegy, in the middle of things (*in medias res*). And, as the poem soon reveals, the epic style of this opening is apt enough – for Ovid says that he is attempting to write an epic poem, a poem in hexameters telling of war and heroes. But in the middle of this noble literary enterprise, Cupid mischievously appears and turns Ovid's epic hexameter into elegiac couplets, turning Ovid simultaneously into an elegiac poet and an elegiac lover (1.1-4; 17-26):

Arms and the violence of war – that was what I was about to
                                                          tell you,
  In heavy hexameter, with subject matching metre.
The second verse was the same as the first – but Cupid laughed,
  So they say, and snatched away one of the feet.

Whenever a new page of poetry starts well with the first line,
  The next line saps my strength.
But I don't have any material suitable for a lighter metre,
  A boy or a girl with lovely long hair.
I was complaining away, when at once he opened his quiver
  And chose the arrows made for my destruction.
Resolutely he bent his curving bow across his knee,
  And said, 'Take that, poet. Here's something to write about.'
Ouch! That boy had dead straight arrows.
  I am on fire, and now Love rules over my empty heart.

Ovid's metre, the elegiac couplet, gives shape, colour, and music to his poetry. And it is the common thread that binds together the themes of his superficially very different elegiac works. Not all of his elegiac 'love songs' are about love – in fact, not all of his self-titled *Loves* are about love – but their shared elegiac metre ties them to the traditions of Latin love elegy. Repeatedly, Ovid tells us that the elegiac couplet was the natural metre of his thought – that when he tried to write prose it came out in elegiac couplets, and when he tried to write in the hexameter of epic, it too came out in elegiac couplets. The elegiac couplet is made up of two lines – the first a long line or *hexameter* made up of six feet, the second a short line or *pentameter* of five feet. In the *Loves*, Ovid describes a meeting with the Muse of Elegy herself, making a joke of this uneven metrical arrangement (*Loves* 3.1.7-10):

> Elegy came, with her curled scented hair,
> > And, I think, one foot longer than the other.
> Her shape was good, her dress tight, her face lovely,
> > And the imperfection of her feet only added to her charm.

Elegy is one of the most ancient forms of poetry, with the earliest extant examples dating from soon after the time of Homer in the seventh century BC. Although it was later to be used by Greek poets concerned with everything from mythology and warfare, through politics and pederasty, to love poems, laments, and drinking songs, elegy was originally associated with grave dedications and funeral epitaphs. In fact, the traditional etymology of the word was considered by the Roman love poets to derive from the Greek '*e legein*', 'to cry woe', and Antimachus, the first Greek poet to produce a collection of elegiac love poetry, dedicated his book to the memory of his dead girlfriend – naming the work, *Lyde*, after her.

The elegiac metre, like all those used in classical Latin poetry, was appropriated from the Greeks but, as with so many of their 'borrowings', the Roman poets fundamentally altered the character of their Greek model and made it their own. The Roman love poet Catullus resisted the structural limitations imposed by the metre, allowing his expressions of emotion to flow across the line-divisions and exploiting the verse form with disjointed sense units to create the effect of a lover writing under emotional strain. His poetic successors continued to develop elegy, but, unlike Catullus, they moved away from the stylistic conventions of Greek elegy as they redefined the characteristics of elegiac mood, style, and subject, to form a new kind of poetry – Latin love elegy. Through the work of these poets – Gallus (of whose writing only brief fragments survive, too little to adequately assess his undoubted influence upon the elegiac genre); Tibullus (to whom Ovid pays tribute in the central poem of Book 3 of the *Loves*); and Propertius (whose direct influence upon Ovid's elegiac writing is perhaps the greatest) – Latin love elegy became recognised as a distinct literary genre. Love had been a key theme in the erotic poetry of the Greeks – particularly the poetry of Sappho, Alcaeus, and Callimachus – and the lyric poetry of Catullus and Horace had explored the highs and lows of love. Now Gallus, Tibullus, Propertius, and Ovid reinvented the role of the poet-lover and made Latin love elegy their own.

These Latin love elegists themselves explicitly describe elegy as a *fallax opus*, a 'deceitful genre' (Propertius 4.1.135). But this description of the genre in which Ovid writes all but one of his major works presents a paradox. If an elegist tells us not to trust elegy, how should we believe him? This paradox becomes particularly troubling when an elegist like Ovid uses his poetry to tell us about his life and loves. How are we to distinguish fact from fiction? Most of what we think we know about Ovid comes from his own elegiac writings. The poems that frame his career, the *Loves* and the exile poems, offer particularly rich sources of 'autobiographical' detail. In these poems, he writes about his family and his friends, his childhood and his education, his tastes in poetry and in women, his work and its reception. And, although all or none of what he tells us may reflect 'reality', we are seduced somehow into believing – or wanting to believe – in the sincerity of the poet's words. This is what Ovid has to say about his life and art in an 'autobiographical' elegy written while in exile (*Sad Songs* 4.10.1-90):

So that you may know who I was – the playful poet of tender love
    Whom you now read – listen you who will come after me.
Sulmo is my homeland, rich in ice-cold streams,
    Ninety miles away from Rome.
Here I was born, and – so that you may know the date –
    It was when both consuls fell to an equal fate.
If it means anything, I inherited my rank from ancient ancestors,
    I was no knight just made by the gift of fortune.
I was not the first son; a brother came first,
    Born twelve months before me.
The same star marked both our births,
    And one birthday was celebrated with two cakes;
The day which belongs to Minerva and her weapons
    And is often the first to be bloody in conflict.
We began our education early and through the care of our father
    We were sent to men of the city, distinguished in the liberal
                                   arts.
My brother inclined towards oratory from a tender age:
    He was born for the forceful weapons of the wordy law
                                     courts.
But for me, even as a boy, divine poetry was a pleasure
    And the Muse kept drawing me to her private work.
Often my father said, 'Why do you bother with such profitless
                                pursuits?
    Even Homer himself left no money.'
I was influenced by his words and, abandoning poetry completely,
    Kept trying to write words free of verse.
But a song would come with its own rhyme
    And whatever I tried to write became poetry.
Meanwhile, the silent passing years slipped by,
    And we brothers put on the toga of adult freedoms,
And our shoulders wore the broad purple stripe,
    But our interests remained as they were before.
And now my brother had seen twenty years of life when

He died – and I lost a part of myself.
I loved and respected the poets of that time.
   All the living poets I regarded as gods.
Often Macer – a grand old man – read to me of his birds,
   And the snakes that kill and the herbs that cure.
Often Propertius would recite his flaming verses
   With the bond of alliance that now joined him to me.
Ponticus famous for his epic, and Bassus for his iambics,
   Were both loving members of my group.
Melodious Horace also held our ears
   While he tuned his fine songs to the Ausonian lyre.
Virgil I only saw, and to Tibullus selfish Fate
   Gave no time for friendship with me.
He was your successor Gallus, and Propertius was his:
   After them, fourth in line, was me.
And as I loved the older poets, so I was loved by the younger ones,
   For my Muse was not slow to win fame.
When I first read my youthful poems in public
   My beard had been cut only once or twice.
My imagination was stirred by a girl whose name was sung
                                        throughout
   The city, and who I called by a false name – Corinna.
I wrote a great deal, but everything I considered less than perfect
   I myself gave to the fire to be edited.
When I was about to go into exile, songs which would have
                                        pleased others,
   I burned: I was angry with my profession and my songs.
My heart was always soft – undefended against Cupid's weapons,
   Moved by the slightest emotion.
And yet, though I was the sort to blaze up at the smallest spark,
   No scandal was ever attached to my name.
When I was little more than a boy I was married to a useless and
                                        worthless
   Woman, who was my wife for only a brief time.

She was followed by one who was blameless,
  But who was not destined to stay my bride.
At last came the one who has stayed with me into my final years
  And has put up with being the wife of an exile.
My young daughter who has borne two children
  (Though not by the same husband) has made me a grand-
                                                father.
My father completed his allotted years,
  Adding forty-five years to his first forty-five.
I wept for him just as he would have wept if I had been taken first.
  Next I buried my mother.
A lucky pair, and their deaths timely,
  Since they died before the day of my punishment.
I too am lucky that my misfortune does not fall
  In their lifetime and they do not grieve for me.
But if anything more than a name remains of those who have died,
  And if a slender shade escapes the funeral pyre,
If, my dear parents, rumours about me have reached your ghosts
  And the charges against me are also heard in the courts of
                                                Hell,
Believe, I beg (and it is a sin to lie to you),
  That the cause of my exile is a mistake and not a crime.

What can we establish about Ovid's life from his poetry? Ovid's literary career probably began in his late teens and continued for over forty years, during which period he produced an extensive body of work. It is possible that the first poems of the *Loves* were begun as early as 25 BC – when Ovid was only eighteen – and first published around 16 BC, with a second edition (the version that we have today) reissued around AD 1. In the meantime, the first volume of the *Heroines' Letters* containing the single letters was written, and it is likely that the first two books of the *Art of Love* also appeared (according to *Loves* 2.18.19), probably around 1 BC.

Published shortly afterwards, his *Cosmetics for Women* – of which only a fragment remains – was followed by the third book of the *Art of Love* and its antidote for unhappy lovers, the *Cures for Love*. This early period of intense literary production was followed by work on Ovid's epic *Metamorphoses* (his only surviving work composed in the hexameter metre of epic) and his elegiac *Calendar*. Work upon these two long poems appears to have been carried out concurrently, and some critics cite the pressure of simultaneous work upon two lengthy and elaborate projects as one of the main reasons for his failure to complete all twelve projected books of the *Calendar* – although, as we shall see, other motivating factors may have exerted greater influence on Ovid's decision to end this project halfway through.

In AD 8 Ovid was banished from Rome to the distant, cold, and miserable town of Tomis on the Black Sea (modern Constanta in Romania) where he continued to write for a further ten years until his death in AD 17 at the age of sixty, producing the elegiac *Sad Songs* and *Letters from Pontus*. Technically and officially, Ovid was punished not with exile (*exsilium*) but with banishment or relegation (*relegatio*) – a more lenient penalty that did not involve the seizure of the poet's financial assets, but did entail the public banning of his works. In *Sad Songs* (2.207-12), he explains the background to his banishment, but does not provide us with any particulars:

> Though two crimes, a song and mistake, have destroyed me,
>   On the cause of the one deed, I have to remain silent.
> For I am not worthy of reopening your wounds, Caesar.
>   It is more than enough that you have been pained once.
> The other charge remains: I am accused of becoming by a
>   shameful song
>   A teacher of obscene adultery.

The offensive song or *carmen* was his *Art of Love*, but Ovid gives us very few clues as to the nature of his mistake or *error*, hinting only that he saw inadvertently something which he should not (*Sad Songs* 2.103-4). The reasons behind the poet's banishment by the emperor Augustus remain a mystery. If it was really the publication of the *Art of Love* that so offended Augustus, as Ovid suggests, then it seems strange that the emperor should wait almost nine years after the poem's publication in 1 BC to punish its author. Augustus' real motive, Ovid implies, was some other unknown offence – often presumed to be a scandal related to the emperor's granddaughter Julia, who was banished from Rome at around the same time as Ovid. But whether or not Ovid was ever 'really' caught up in any serious affair concerning Julia, and whether or not Augustus was ever 'really' offended by the immorality of the 'obscene' *Art of Love* – we will never know.

However, biographical details can only tell us so much about a poet and his poetry, and it can be misleading to reconstruct a life narrative on the basis of what a poet may choose to tell us about his life experiences in his work. Such reconstructions, admittedly, are particularly seductive in Ovid's case, as his elegiac writing frequently invites an autobiographical style of reading. But Ovid's writing belongs to a *fallax opus*. Ovid claims, for example, that he began to give public performances reciting poems about his love affair with Corinna – that is, his *Loves* – when his beard had been cut only once or twice. This may be a direct reference to Ovid's life, or it may be a literary allusion to art, for the Greek poet Callimachus also claimed to have been *artigeneios* (with his beard just beginning to grow) when he first embarked upon his poetic career. Or it may be both. In this case, any potential gap between fact and fiction seems relatively unimportant. But when Ovid tells us about the death of his older brother when he was nineteen, describing how he 'lost a part' of himself with that loss, we might feel very differently about the poet and his work if we were to learn that this was untrue – that Ovid never had a brother, or that he lived to a ripe old age, for example. Sometimes we mind the gap between fact and fiction.

Ovid constructs a vivid poetic persona in his elegiac writings, one we can imagine acting out the scenes he describes, and speaking to us directly of his real lived experiences, his loves, and his sorrows. But Ovid also reminds us that 'Ovid' is an artistic construction and a literary persona no less than a living person. It is worth noting too that Ovid – or, to give him his full tripartite 'equestrian' name, Publius Ovidius Naso – always identifies himself in his poetry as 'Naso'. Naso or 'the Nose' is a shared family nickname, which is always used by Ovid the poet, the lover, and the exile in his elegiac writings because this part of his name (unlike Publius or Ovidius) neatly fits the elegiac metre. It can be helpful to remember that Ovid, or Naso, similarly chooses all other aspects of his poetic auto-biography, selecting those details that accord with the conventions and traditions of elegy – and omitting or suppressing those that do not. Whenever Ovid speaks of himself in the first person or says 'I' in the elegies, that *ego* is not necessarily or always offering us an autobiographical confession. As we shall see.

1

Loves

humansong [hoo'-mun-sahng] n. a song sung to convince someone to love you. As human beings evolved, people discovered that singing was a way to seduce people they had crushes on. It began awkwardly, with out-of-tune guitars from teenage years dragged up from basements, and embarrassed singers recording their songs and sending them to the desired person through the postal system without explanation or return address. With time, instruments fell out of use, and people began to risk singing their songs in person, mostly unaccompanied, even though their faces sometimes turned red, as did the faces of the people they sang to ... The success of the humansong was so great that other, less successful human mating rituals like small talk, alcohol consumption, and bad dancing were abandoned in favor of singing. Every humansong is as unique as a fingerprint or snowflake.

Nicole Krauss, *The Future Dictionary of America*

If the 'humansong' is as unique as a fingerprint, signifying both individuality and originality, the love song is a footprint, marking a well-trodden path along which many have gone before us. As Duncan Kennedy has put it, when we articulate our love for another person, 'it is disconcerting to feel that the phrase "I love you" may have emerged from our mouths already equipped with inverted commas, that we may have been acting out a script that has been played out, with much the same plot and much the same words, by many before us'. When we say, sing, or write to another 'I love you', however sincerely, we are speaking from a well-rehearsed script; in Roland Barthes' phrase, 'a lover's discourse' speaks through us. For Ovid, too, lovers learn love like a script. In the *Art of Love,* he takes the elegiac equivalent of the phrase 'I love you' – '*tu mihi sola places*' ('you alone please me / you are the only one for me') – and he equips it with inverted commas, claiming that 'you choose to whom you say "I love you"' (1.42). You do not say 'I love you' because you love someone: you love someone because it is to him or her that you say 'I love you'. Similarly, in the *Amores* or *Loves,* Ovid tells us that he is not in love with anyone: there is no one individual he desires or wants to seduce with his love songs. But he recognises the classic symptoms of love – he is aching, restless, and unable to sleep (*Loves* 1.2.1-8). He recognises these signs from the descriptions of love offered by those who have loved before him: this is how someone in love *acts* – therefore, he must be in love and now he must find someone to *play the part* of his lover.

That 'player' is Corinna, the romantic and erotic focus of Ovid's *amor* and of his *Amores.* His relationship with this mysterious woman provides the framework around which he arranges the three books of his first love songs. Book 1 narrates the start of their affair and details the poet-lover's infatuation with his new girl-friend; Book 2 covers the mid-point of their increasingly rocky relationship, detailing Ovid's jealousies and Corinna's infidelities; and Book 3 describes the breakdown and eventual break-up of the affair – the end of Ovid's love corresponding with the end of his book of *Loves.* Ovid sometimes hints that the woman he calls 'Corinna' is a married woman of some rank and status, but also suggests that she could be a courtesan or *meretrix,* even alluding to her as a 'whore'. She is beautiful but vain, clever but calculating, jealous but unfaithful, passionate but cruel – the stereotypical elegiac girlfriend, just like Propertius' Cynthia, or Tibullus' Delia. In fact, Corinna conforms to the pattern of elegiac *domina* or *puella* so well that it seems naïve to think there might be a woman behind the pseudonym; as with Dylan's 'Corinna', it seems unnecessary to ask who Ovid's Corinna 'really' might have been. Yet, in *Loves* 3.12, Ovid complains that his poems in praise of Corinna's beauty and charms have made other men want her too and that now he feels like a 'pimp'. He reminds his readers that poets make things up: a gentle caution both that Corinna's beauty and charms may not 'really' be as he has described them in his love songs – and a reminder that Corinna herself may have been 'made up', manufactured (or 'womanufactured') by Ovid's imagination and pen (3.12.7-12; 43f):

> Am I wrong, or have my poetry books made her notorious?
>> That will be it – my own literary genius has made her a
>>> whore.
> And I deserve it! Why was I advertising her beauty?
>> It's my own fault that the girl I love is now for sale.
> I am the pimp; I am the henchman who has led in the lover,
>> My right hand has opened her door.
>
> You ought to have seen that my compliments about my woman
>> were false.
>> Now your gullibility is my undoing.

Ovid again mocks the gullibility of some of his readers in the third book of the *Art of Love*, when he tells us that among his contemporaries 'there are many who ask who my Corinna is' (3.538) – echoing his claim in the *Loves* that (2.17.28-30):

> There are many women who would like to make a name
>> through me.
> I know one girl who spreads it around that she is Corinna.
>> What wouldn't she give to make it so?

His teasing here is full of sexual innuendo. And when he tells us about the girl who 'spreads it around that she is Corinna' and suggestively comments that she would 'give' him anything – including herself – to make it so, he is suggesting that 'Corinna' might be *any* girl with whom he chooses to have sex. In fact – with a motif that resonates throughout the *Loves* – he claims that there are 'many' women (*multae*) who would like to play Corinna's part and take her name. Yet, in the same poem, he also seems to pledge his fidelity to Corinna as 'the one' for him (2.17.33f):

> I will sing of *none* but you in my little books;
> You *alone* will be the inspiration to my genius.

Ovid appears to be making the point that, of all the women that he might choose to call 'Corinna' and to make his *amor*, he has singled out this *one* woman. But in the broader context of the poem, his pledge of love and devotion, his implicit performance of the script that declares 'she is the *one* for him', can be read as a lightly veiled threat. If 'Corinna' does not mend her ways and treat her lover with more tenderness and respect, if she does not try to love him as he loves her, then there are plenty of other women out there to whom Ovid can say in her place *'you are the one for me'*.

In *Loves* 1.3, Ovid similarly seeks to assure his new *puella* – who has not yet been identified or given a name – of his fidelity and his undying devotion (1.3.15f; 25f):

> I don't tell all the girls that they are 'the one'; I don't leap from
>   love to love.
>   Trust me, you will be my heart's desire forever.

> People throughout the whole world will sing about the two of us
>   together,
>   And my name will be joined to yours forever.

But, already alerted to the potential for deception in this elegy by the poet's request to 'trust me' (remembering that elegy is a self-confessed *fallax opus*), Ovid's declaration of lifelong devotion to one girl sounds suspiciously insincere. He swears that her name and his will be joined together forever – *but this girl has no name*. The name 'Corinna' does not appear in Ovid's *Loves* until poem 1.5 and we are offered nothing in the context of the elegy itself to help us identify this anonymous 'girl'. As Duncan Kennedy suggests, the poem and Ovid's declaration of love reads like a pro-forma upon which any girl can fill in her name in the blank space provided – providing she is prepared to love and in turn be loved. Ovid can 'sincerely' offer eternal fame and lifelong devotion to this *one* girl, because she is potentially *any* and *all* of the girls that he might ever desire.

Again, as if to illustrate (with obvious irony) that Corinna is only one of the many girls to whom Ovid chooses to say '*tu mihi sola places*' – 'you are the *one* for me' – several of his love poems explicitly refer to erotic encounters with other women. He offers two separate accounts of how he fell in love at first sight – once at the temple of Apollo (2.2.3ff), and another time at the Circus (3.2) – indicating that at least one of these 'love' affairs must have overlapped with his relationship with Corinna. And in a poem supposedly describing Ovid's experience of sexual impotence he boasts about recent sexual encounters with three named women in addition to the unnamed *puella* whom he has just disappointed (3.7). *Loves* 2.4, however, offers a poetic *tour de force* in its illustration of Ovid's 'amorous' promiscuity and the many women he loves. Eliding his poetic *Loves* with his sexual desires, Ovid gives us a comprehensive list of all the different types of women who turn him on, claiming that (2.4.9f):

> There's no particular kind of beauty that inspires my *loves*.
> And there are a hundred reasons why I'm always in love.

He goes on to tell us that he loves modest girls who look shy, virgins who look like a challenge *and* sexy flirts who look as if they will be easy to get into bed. He loves educated women and simple girls; women who praise his poetry and women who criticise it; he loves women who sing, women who play the lyre, and women who dance; he loves tall women, short women, well-dressed and scruffy women; he loves white girls and he loves black girls; he loves blondes and brunettes, young girls and older women. Ovid was the original 'man who loved women'. He claims explicitly that his *amores* (both his poetry and his passions) are inspired by all these different women, and that – in a corruption of the elegiac lover's declaration '*tu mihi sola places*' – each one of these women 'pleases' him, each one is '*the one*' for him.

So how does Corinna fit in to this list? Of the forty-nine elegies in the *Loves*, Corinna is identified by name in only twelve. We imagine that she is the woman addressed as *puella* and *domina* in the rest of the collection, encouraged to do so by the elegiac lover's discourse which expects its performers to play to and with only one leading lady. But Corinna is only one of Ovid's many women. In his poem purporting to tell of the poet's experience of sexual dysfunction, he claims unashamedly of recent 'love-ins' with at least three other women, unusually identified by name – perhaps to lend authenticity to his boast (3.7.23-6):

> Yet recently I satisfied blonde Chlide twice with my attentions,
>   The beautiful Pitho three times, and Libas three times too;
> I remember Corinna demanding from me and me delivering
>   Nine lots in one short night.

Appropriately, the key to understanding Ovid's love for Corinna may lie in her name. Corinna shares the Greek styling of her name with the other mistresses of Roman love poetry, yet one key characteristic of this pseudonym distinguishes her from those other elegiac women – and, at the same time, identifies her as an 'everywoman'. While the names of Lycoris, Delia, and Cynthia (respectively loved by Gallus, Tibullus, and Propertius) each allude to cult names associated with Apollo, god of poetry, Corinna draws her pseudonym from a 'real' woman – the Greek love poet Korinna. And, in an ingenious bilingual wordplay depending upon his original Roman audience's knowledge of Greek, Ovid's use of the name 'Corinna' as the sobriquet for his girlfriend plays on the Greek word for 'girl' – *kore*: a word that is also equivalent to the Latin *puella*. When Ovid sings of 'Corinna' then, he is effectively singing of 'a girl'; the name he gives to his girlfriend is the name of 'Girlfriend'. Or, translated into twenty-first century terms, perhaps 'Baby' – the name of the 'girl' who has inspired a thousand modern love songs, the name you can use with each and any of your lovers, and the name that allowed Westlife and Busted to sing straight to the hearts of a million loving teenage female fans.

For Ovid then, the name of 'Corinna' provides a blank space in the script of his lover's discourse into which any and every girl can read her own name; and into which every reader can choose to project the name of 'the one'. There is no 'flesh and blood' Corinna whose true identity is clothed by the pseudonym. In *Loves* 1.5, the elegy in which Ovid first introduces Corinna by name, the naked truth of this is revealed in tantalising detail:

> It was hot, and the day had passed its middle hour.
>> I lay my body in the middle of the bed to rest.
> One shutter was open, the other was closed, giving
>> The kind of light that woods have;
> The kind of twilight that glows when the sun sets,
>> Or when the night has passed but the day has not yet begun.

That is the kind of light to offer to shy girls,
    In which their timid modesty can hope to find a hiding
                        place.
Look! Corinna comes, wearing an unbelted tunic,
    Her parted hair touching her pale neck,
Just as they say lovely Semiramis looked going into her bedroom,
    Or Thais loved by so many men.
I tore off her dress. It was thin so wasn't much ripped.
    Still, she fought to cover herself with it.
But because she fought like someone who doesn't really want to
                        win,
    She was easily beaten in her own surrender.
As she stood undressed before my eyes,
    I saw there was no mark on her whole body.
Such shoulders, such arms I saw and I felt.
    Her breasts just asking to be touched.
So smooth the belly beneath that perfect bosom.
    So long and lovely her sides. So youthful her thigh.
Why should I list everything? I saw nothing to complain about,
    And I pressed her naked body to mine.
Who doesn't know the rest? Worn out, we both slept.
    My middays – let them often turn out this way.

This erotically charged poem is unlike anything written by Ovid's elegiac predecessors. Here, for the first time, we seem to see an elegiac *puella* 'in the flesh'. As the poet's eyes move slowly down the woman's naked body, we see her shoulders, arms, and breasts, her belly, thighs, and legs – before they fall into bed together. The poem seems incredibly daring in its erotic subject and its intimate representation of the female form. But look again. Nothing distinctive is revealed about Corinna in this poetic striptease. Her perfect body bears no mark, and Ovid's description uses only the blandest of adjectives to represent it: her body is smooth, flawless, slender, beautiful, young – idealised and unreal. There is nothing about this girl to set her apart from any other idealised elegiac *puella*. What is more, the poet draws a discreet veil over the couple just as they are about to make love, modestly avoiding any direct reference to sex. And in the same way, he discreetly moves his gaze – and that of his readers – directly from Corinna's belly to her thighs, modestly avoiding any direct reference to *her* sex. We see Corinna only in fragments; we never see her whole. There is a blank space in the middle of this poem; a space defined by Corinna's body.

Although *Loves* 1.5 is often commended by post-Romantic readers for its humour, its candidly eroticised view of love and its explicit representation of sex, its poetic striptease is far from revealing. The *appearance* of openness, sincerity, and candour in this poem serves as an effective cover for the artifice and dissimu-lation that lie beneath. The explicit and detailed representation of Corinna's body in this poem – the careful anatomisation of her arms and breasts, her stomach and legs – distracts us from the fact that this woman is composed of parts: that she is 'made up'. Moreover, the scene in which this erotic performance is played out is artfully arranged: the soft-focus lighting spotlights the lovers' bed upon which Ovid, our male lead, is centrally positioned; Corinna enters dramatically, and 'playfully' struggles to retain her modesty as Ovid 'playfully' fights to remove her dress; the indi-vidual parts of her naked body are appraised; and then the scene is suddenly cut. John Barsby suggests that the poet's technique here 'is exactly that of the film, which enjoys a certain amount of nakedness and preliminary love-play but then cuts to the shot of the couple relaxed in bed after the action is over'. We could also say that the poet's technique in this erotic scene explicitly represents love – and sex – as a performance. Both Ovid and Corinna in this poem are playing roles. They do not speak, but their actions seem nevertheless to have been scripted as part of the elegiac lover's discourse.

This aspect of the poem is perhaps most dramatically demonstrated in the 'playful' violence that takes place between Ovid and Corinna. Eroticised violence and fights between lovers (or as Paul Veyne describes them, 'Venus' battles') are a prominent feature of Latin love elegy and appear in several of Ovid's love songs. As in *Loves* 1.5, the rules of engagement are usually straightforward: the elegiac *puella* puts up a 'fight', refusing to give herself to the elegiac lover, but his desire is aroused all the more by her show of resistance, so he 'fights' back until she is 'defeated'. Although the violence can sometimes go too far, occasionally allowing someone to get 'really' hurt (as Ovid tells us in *Loves* 1.7), the emphasis in these 'battles' is always upon pretence and dissimulation – on feinting rather than fighting. Yet, such 'fights' do more than add sadomasochistic spice to the elegiac love affair; they act out two of the genre's most potent and pervasive tropes – the idea of love both as a kind of warfare (*militia amoris*) and as a kind of slavery (*servitium amoris*). In *Loves* 1.2, Ovid combines these two elegiac tropes and imagines himself surrendering to Cupid as a prisoner of war might give himself up to the leader of a conquering army (1.2.17-22):

> The unwilling are more bitterly and more fiercely pressed
>   Than those who admit their own slavery to Love.
> So, look, I admit it! I am your latest prisoner of war, Cupid.
>   I stretch out my hands to be tied, under your command.
> There's no need for war – I ask for peace and release.
>   There will be no glory for you in conquering an unarmed
>   man.

In a later poem, describing himself in bed with Corinna in his arms, Ovid again draws upon the trope of *militia amoris* when he imagines himself no longer as a prisoner but as a military general serving in Cupid's army (2.12). He celebrates his victory over the enemy forces – Corinna's husband, her guardian, and her front door – and he takes pride in having defeated his enemy and having seized his objective without bloodshed. That is, he enjoys the fiction rather than the 'reality' of fighting in one of 'Venus' battles'. But the gap between fiction and reality here reminds us that the roles of 'soldier' and 'slave' are not simply parts that the elegiac *lover* plays. We are reminded rather that, like the parts of 'soldier' and 'slave', the role of 'lover' itself is also a part in the performance of 'love': the lover does not represent the 'reality' behind the 'fiction' of soldier or slave. Similarly, we should not see the dominated *puella* – who is always 'defeated' in these play fights – as representing the 'reality' behind the 'fiction' of elegiac *domina*: both 'victim' and 'mistress' are roles scripted by the elegiac lover's discourse.

This duplicity in elegiac role-playing is foregrounded in a pair of poems dealing explicitly with the motif of sex and slavery – and of sex *as* slavery. In *Loves* 2.7 and 2.8, Ovid introduces us to a character who also knows Corinna as a *domina*, her slave Cypassis. In the first of the paired elegies, he swears – 'by Venus and Cupid' (the elegiac equivalent of crossing his fingers) – that Corinna is wrong to accuse him of sleeping with her slave. He tries to illustrate the foolishness of the charge by intimating that Cypassis, Corinna's talented hairdresser, is a more valuable slave to her mistress than he, her elegiac *servus*. He knows that good hairdressers and slaves are hard to find but lovers are not, and to make a move upon Cypassis would risk his rejection by both slave and mistress. Corinna's accusations of infidelity, Ovid complains, are as absurd as they are unjust. But in the second of the paired poems, the poet reveals that, just as Corinna suspected, he has been sleeping with her slave girl. Here, though,

Ovid identifies himself explicitly as a *dominus* and threatens the slave Cypassis with the exposure of their affair if she will not repay him 'in kind' for his discretion and his deception – as evidenced in the previous poem – suggesting that the slave should try to please at least one of her masters (2.8.24). In this (doubled) *ménage à trois*, Ovid is able to play the parts of both *servus* and *dominus*, reminding us of his own flexibility in performing the role of elegiac lover, but also exposing the mutability of other elegiac roles and the relationships between them. For, in the context of these poems, it is clearly not enough to claim that Ovid is 'really' the *dominus* who holds ultimate power over the two women, and that he is never 'really' a slave – that one of these is a role and the other not.

It is possible, admittedly, to detect here and in the elegiac tropes of *militia amoris* and *servitium amoris* – particularly in the eroticised violence of 'Venus' battles' – a dark note of misogyny. When love is presented as warfare and the bed as a battlefield, the elegiac woman quickly becomes a casualty, a captive, or a trophy. As in *Loves* 1.5, the idealised *puella* can easily become objectified, and the beloved *domina* can be humiliated by her 'slave' – ostensibly showing us the 'reality' of their relationship, in which *he* dominates sexually, socially, and physically and in which *she* is dominated.

But Ovid's treatment of these elegiac figures is more complicated than this model of misogyny allows. To take the trope of *servitium amoris* first, Ovid's representation of the relationship between himself and his *domina* discloses an intricate power play in operation between the two figures. Corinna, like so many Roman women, Ovid reveals in *Loves* 1.14, used to colour her hair. But, with cosmetics and colouring products somewhat less reliable in the first century BC than they are today, her hair falls out. As she sits crying before her mirror, holding her lost hair in her lap, Ovid demonstrates a marked lack of sympathy for his lover's distress. He recalls the former glory of the hair and the sexual desire that it aroused in him, 'depersonalising' Corinna as he does so. He attributes her (former) beauty to her long hair rather than to Corinna herself – just as he objectified her beauty in *Loves* 1.5 by cataloguing and anatomising the erotic parts of her body. In this poem, however, Ovid goes further, depersonalising Corinna through the personification of her hair. He imagines her delicate tresses suffering daily torture, patiently enduring 'iron' and 'fire' in order to be curled into ringlets, he berates Corinna herself for her 'iron-hearted' cruelty, and he laments that her beautiful hair has 'died' (1.14.23-31). His personification sees Corinna's hair as a *servus*, enduring hot curling irons as a Roman slave might endure the instruments of torture – or as an elegiac lover (a *slave* to love) might endure the cruelty and 'torture' meted out to him by his 'iron-hearted' mistress.

The architect of her own misfortune, Corinna herself is pictured in elegiac terms as her own jealous rival or as a treacherous witch, poisoned or cursed by her own hand (1.14.39-44). Combining the elegiac tropes of *militia* and *servitium amoris*, she is also figured as a prisoner of war, bowing her head and offering up her hair to her Roman conqueror as a symbol of her submission and defeat, while the victorious Ovid taunts her that she will now have to wear a wig – and, what is more, a wig made from the hair of a captive German woman. The loss of her hair has entailed the loss of Corinna's desirability and therefore the loss of her status as Ovid's beloved: like the slave whose hair she will have to wear, Ovid's *domina* has become a casualty, a captive, and a war trophy in the war that is waged between the lines of Latin love elegy. Meanwhile, echoes from Ovid's earliest poems in the *Loves* help to make Corinna's defeat explicit. In *Loves* 1.1, he called for 'a girl with lovely long hair' (1.1.20) to provide him with material for his love poetry: now that girl is bald and holds her lovely long hair in her lap – a striking image of humiliation.

Yet, Ovid's representations of his *domina*'s domination and defeat in this poem are far from straightforward. The opening line of the poem – 'I kept telling you, "stop dyeing your hair!" ' – can be read as a triumphant shout of vindication, a patronising 'I told you so!' and a declaration affirming the poet's superiority over his vain mistress. Or it can be read as a cry of frustration and a sign that Ovid's repeated efforts to dominate and control this woman have themselves been in vain. Corinna has clearly resisted his attempts to determine her appearance (albeit with unfortunate consequences) and this evidence of her independence is significant. In fact, we might see in the poet's struggle to offer an adequate description of his beloved's hair – particularly its colour – evidence that she has successfully frustrated his attempts to determine her and her representation in his elegiac writing. The poet tries to describe the colour of her hair as 'not black, but not golden', but nor is it 'in-between' either (1.14.9f): the hair that we are led to imagine Corinna has dyed many times and perhaps many different colours seems to resist the poet's precise description, as Corinna herself resists easy definition. Like her hair, she too proves – if not 'docile' – certainly 'suited to a hundred styles' (1.14.13). But Corinna's varied hair colour may remind us that Ovid, as he himself tells us, is both attracted to and 'suited to' *women* of various styles – including women with black hair and golden hair (2.4.39-43). Corinna, with her hair that is neither exactly black nor precisely golden, may represent all of these women – or perhaps none. And, though she may have been humiliated and defeated in *Loves* 1.14, the poem ends with Ovid showing 'mercy' and making 'peace' with his beloved, offering the reassurance that her own hair will very soon grow back. Soon she will again be the object of his desire, the subject of his love poetry, and the recursive power play between the two lovers can begin all over again.

2

The Art of Love

The grammar of Love's Art
Ovid still teaches,
Grotesque in Pontic snows
And bearskin breeches.

'Let man be ploughshare,
Woman his field;
Flatter, beguile, assault,
And she must yield.'

'Snatch the morning rose
Fresh from the wayside,
Deflower it in haste
Ere the dew be dried.'

Ovid instructs you how
Neighbours' lands to plough;
'Love smacks the sweeter
For a broken vow.'
                    Robert Graves, 'Ovid in Defeat'

Robert Graves, writing in 1925, offers a neat synthesis of Ovid's erotic teachings in the *Ars Amatoria*, or *Art of Love*. In a parodic abbreviation of the (parodic) farming imagery employed in the *Art of Love*, Graves condenses Ovid's advice to would-be lovers in Books 1 and 2 of the poem to three terse stanzas. Five couplets, highlighted as paraphrase by quotation marks, seem sufficient to express the substance of the poem's first two books. The elegant compression of ideas in epigrammatic style, the parodic use of metaphor, and the play of wit, moreover, lend a characteristic 'Ovidian' quality to Graves' poem. But these 'Ovidian' precepts are not always as they appear. The exhortation in Graves' poem for the would-be lover to 'Flatter, beguile, assault' the object of his desire seems to represent a fair condensation of similar teachings in the *Art of Love* – particularly the precepts outlined in Book 1.619-78, in which Ovid advises a putative lover to employ flattery (1.619-30), false promises (1.631-63), and force (1.664-78) in order to win the object of his affections. In particular, the tension in the reworking of this last piece of advice subtly highlights the aggressive power play implicit in the poem's recommendation that physical 'force' or *uis* may legitimately and successfully be used as a strategy for seduction. The forceful tenor of Graves' couplet – 'Flatter, beguile, assault, / And she *must* yield' – reminds us that, in this context, the lover's application of such force unequivocally implies rape.

Some of the other precepts presented here, however, have no Ovidian source. In particular, the idea that the lover should 'Snatch the morning rose' and 'Deflower it in haste' has no obvious parallel in the *Art of Love*. On the contrary, Ovid advises his pupils that it is not young virgins but older women who make the best lovers, endorsing this personal preference with an elaborate conceit (2.695-700). And, far from advocating hasty defloration, the poem repeatedly recommends a gentle pace for both sex and seduction. According to Ovid (2.717f), 'the pleasure of love should not be hurried, but gradually enticed by slow delay'. The advice highlighted in Graves' fourth stanza focuses upon the contentious view that Ovid advises his pupils on how to commit adultery: 'Ovid instructs you how / Neighbours' lands to plough'. Here, Graves refuses to accept Ovid's own emphatic disclaimer that the *Art of Love* does not teach or condone adultery (1.31-4):

> Keep away, slender headbands, signs of chastity,
>   And the long skirt which covers the feet in its folds.
> I tell of safe sex and permissible cheating,
>   And in my poem there will be no crime.

Yet although, as Roy Gibson notes, Ovid occasionally 'sails especially close to the wind' and even appears explicitly to challenge Augustan laws criminalizing adultery at 3.611-58, Graves' synthesis of Ovid's advice on adultery is misleading. The poem does not explicitly give instruction on how to commit adultery nor 'how / Neighbours' lands to plough' – although Ovid does hint that this may be a temptation to his pupils and readers (1.347-50):

> But why should you be mistaken, since it is new pleasures that
>   are pleasing
>   And since what is another's captivates us more than our
>   own?
> The grass is always greener in another's fields,
>   And the neighbour's herd has bigger udders.

Ovid may also be seen to argue the point that 'Love smacks the sweeter / For a broken vow' in Book 3 of the *Art of Love*, when he advises women to encourage and excite their lovers with the pretence that they are committing adultery, suggesting that the fear of detection will add a little spice to their sex lives (3.589-610). But the emphasis in this passage, as elsewhere, is upon the presentation of a convincing *imitation* of adultery, rather than a convincing *invitation* actually to commit adultery. In the *Art of Love*, image is everything – and, in a poem which professes to teach lovers how to fake everything, nothing can be taken at face value.

Ovid himself insists repeatedly both in the *Art of Love* and in the poems from exile that his poem on the art of seduction and sex was not intended to be taken seriously. In the *Sad Songs*, writing in defence of his provocative poem (1.9.61-2; 2.354), he refers to the *Art of Love* as a game (*lusum*) and a joke (*iocus*), downplaying the didactic seriousness of the work and highlighting its playfulness. Perhaps we should expect nothing else from a banished poet defending his writing and his reputation from the sad shores of the Black Sea, yet the same rhetoric appears in the *Art of Love* itself. Ovid describes the poem in Book 2 (2.600) as 'his little joke' (*nostri ioci*) and draws Book 3 to a close with the declaration that 'the game is over' (*lusus habet finem*).

In emphasising the light-hearted playfulness of the *Art of Love* in this way, Ovid confuses its identification as a serious or straight-forward work of didactic poetry. In the ancient literary world, didactic poetry was traditionally seen as a variation or sub-genre of epic, composed in hexameter verse, treating serious themes in a serious way. But Ovid's *Art of Love* subverts this tradition in its choice of erotic subject and elegiac metre, and in its playful spirit. Ovid's advice on dating, cosmetics, and fashion seems to have more in common with the advice offered in modern men's maga-zines, such as *FHM,* than with the didactic works of other classical writers. Philip Terry's story *Void* explicitly draws out the parallels between Ovid's *Art of Love* and contemporary magazine articles offering tips on dating and sex. In a free translation of *Art of Love* 1.41-60, he reworks for a contemporary readership Ovid's advice on where to look for women:

2. The Art of Love

Tesco's

If in search of a partner, don't despair. Remember: there are plenty of available women at large, and tracking them down won't be hard. It can be enjoyable too. The aisles at Tesco's are as good as any to begin talent spotting: normally there's always something very tasty on display. A man in search of a lover can look nowhere better. Rich rewards are certain. As swarming bees fill parks and playing fields, hovering over the clover, bobbing from dandelion to dandelion, so girls swarm to Tesco's in crowds.

In keeping with the didactic literary tradition – and sometimes in parody of it – Ovid insists that a successful lover, like a successful farmer, philosopher, or poet, must be trained and educated (*doctus*) in his craft (*ars*) so that with experience and practice he – or she – may become a skilled and accomplished (*cultus*) expert. Declaring himself to be an experienced expert in the art of seduction and sex, offering hot sex-tips based on his own first-hand experience, Ovid formally configures the relationship between himself and his readers as that of teacher and pupil, and he adopts for himself the persona of *praeceptor amoris* (professor of love) or *magister amoris* (teacher of love).

According to the precepts of the *Art of Love*, a good lover is not born but made, and good sex requires more than simply 'doing what comes naturally'. So, in the introduction to his *Art of Love*, Ovid writes (1.1-8):

If there is anyone in this city who does not know the art of loving,
    Let him read this poem and, having read it, love like an
                                                            expert.
It is with expertise that swift ships are propelled by sail and oar,
    It is with expertise that fast chariots are driven – and love
                                                            managed.

Automedon was good with chariots and pliant reins,
　　Tiphys was the captain on the Haemonian ship:
I have been appointed by Venus as master of the art of Love.
　　I will be called the Tiphys and Automedon of Love.

Here, Ovid clearly signals that this is to be an erotodidactic poem
– a 'manual', not on sailing, driving, or farming but on sex. Yet the
ground over which Ovid's didactic Muse drives the *Art of Love* is
familiar elegiac territory. The character-types, situations, and
themes of the *Art of Love* are immediately recognisable to readers
of Ovid's *Loves* as the stuff of Roman love elegy, reworked and represented in a new erotodidactic context.

　　Among the many scenes and situations imported from the *Loves*
into the *Art of Love*, Ovid's account of meeting his *puella* at a party
in *Loves* 1.4 offers a fine example of the way in which the poet
experiments with a familiar elegiac topic in a new didactic context.
In the *Loves* poem, Ovid is due to attend a party to which his girlfriend (who may or may not be Corinna) and her husband have
also been invited. Ovid offers detailed advice to his *puella* on how
she should behave in this awkward situation (1.4.13-20, 31f):

Arrive before your husband – I can't see what we can do,
　　If you do arrive before him, but anyway, arrive before him.
When he reclines on the couch, go with him to lie down,
　　Looking like a good girl – but secretly touch my foot.
Watch me and my nods and my body language.
　　Catch my secret signs and answer them with your own.
I'll speak to you with my eyes and brows, speaking soundless words.
　　You'll read words from my fingers, words traced in wine.

The cup you put down, I will be the first to pick up,
　　And from the same part where you have drunk, I too will
　　　　　　　　　　　　　　　　　　　　　　　　　　drink.

2. The Art of Love

In the *Art of Love*, Ovid's instructions are directed not at his girl-friend but at a male pupil facing the same tricky situation. He is instructed (1.571-6) how:

> To trace tender flatteries in light wine,
>> So that on the table she may read how she is your mistress;
> And you should gaze into her eyes with eyes that confess passion;
>> Often a silent look has voice and words.
> Make sure that you are the first to seize the wine glass touched by
>> her lips,
>> And drink from that same part from which she has drunk.

The situations and instructions in these two scenarios may seem identical, yet the tone adopted in the didactic *Art of Love* is very different from that found in the elegiac *Loves*. In the *Loves*, according to the conventions of love elegy, the lover-poet fears that, even if she follows his instructions during the party, his mistress will 'betray' him by going home with her husband at the end of the night. With comic pathos, he prays that if she does then sleep with her husband she will do so unwillingly, and will take no pleasure in it – in essence, he prays that she will not achieve orgasm. Finally, he begs that, if she does sleep with her husband (and if she does enjoy it), the next day she will lie to her lover and steadfastly promise him that she withheld her sexual favours (1.4.69f):

> But, no matter what, whatever happens to happen later that night,
>> Tomorrow, promise me with sincere tones that you did not
>>> give in.

The wry, self-deprecating humour of this poem is very different from the cynical, calculating tone of the parallel scene in the *Art*

47

of Love. The lover-poet of the *Loves* assumes that his instructions to his *puella* will ultimately prove useless and that he will end the night sleeping alone. The instructor of the *Art of Love* assumes that his scheming plans will be successful and that his pupil will end the night by 'taking care' of the girl in the place of her drunken husband. Unlike the poet-lover of *Loves* 1.4, the reader and pupil of the *Art of Love* does not expect to end up sleeping alone. There is certainly a note of cynicism in the lover-poet's plea that his mistress lie to him about having sex with her husband, but the self-deception implied here contrasts markedly with the calculated deception and manipulation of mistress and husband in the *Art of Love.*

It is important to notice, then, that although Ovid deals with the same erotic themes in both the *Loves* and *Art of Love*, his approach to this material is fundamentally different. The elegiac poet-lover – the principal player in Ovid's *Loves* – offers a view of love and sex that is personal, subjective, and pessimistic. The didactic *praeceptor amoris* – the poet and professor of love in the *Art of Love* – offers a very different perspective upon love and sex. His view is necessarily impersonal, objective, and optimistic: after all, he professes to teach the art of successful seduction to anyone who does not already know how. And, whereas the dominant disposition of the elegiac poet-lover is that of erotic frustration, despairing at his lover's infidelities, lamenting her hard-heartedness, the pose of the didactic *magister amoris* or teacher of love conversely assumes a successful sexual history in which the hard heart of his *puella* was softened and seduced. Indeed, it is precisely this history of erotic success on which the didactic poet bases his authority and expertise as a teacher.

In the second book of the *Art of Love*, this characteristic feature of didactic poetry – the author's claim to teach others from his own first-hand experience – takes on another dimension, as Ovid draws a direct link between his didactic expertise as a teacher in the arts of love and his elegiac experiences as a love poet in the *Loves*. In *Loves* 1.7, Ovid describes an incident in which he himself violently assaults an unnamed girlfriend (often presumed to be Corinna), tearing at her hair and scratching her face. While modern readers may be uncomfortable with such material, similar accounts of violence against a lover are not uncommon in Roman love elegy. Propertius and Tibullus also write about similarly violent incidents in which they have ripped clothes, torn out hair, and bruised their girlfriends' eyes and cheeks. The light-hearted tone of Ovid's retelling of this elegiac scenario, moreover, has suggested to some readers that the assault described in the *Loves* is a fiction, a witty reworking of a disturbing elegiac trope in which the distraught poet-lover beseeches the shocked victim of his violent abuse to hit him back – or at least to put her hair up again and pretend that nothing has happened (1.7.63-8):

> But don't hold back – your revenge will lessen my own pain.
>> Now go at my face with your nails.
> Don't spare my eyes or my hair.
>> Although your hand is weak, anger will give it strength.
> Or at least, so that the sad evidence of my crime is destroyed,
>> Put up your hair again as it was arranged before.

In the *Art of Love*, however, Ovid appeals directly to this 'real-life' experience of one of 'Venus' battles' in order to teach his pupils a valuable lesson: not that they should restrain themselves from assaulting their girlfriends because of any moral imperative, but rather because they will have to pay dearly for any such outburst of violent temper (2.169-74):

I remember how once, in anger, I tore my mistress' hair:
  How many days did that anger steal from me!
I don't think that I tore her dress; I didn't notice it; but she
  Said I had, and the dress was repaired at my expense.
So you, if you are sensible, avoid your teacher's mistakes,
  And avoid the cost that my slip-up caused.

The cynical twist that Ovid puts upon his retelling of this event is characteristic of his treatment of elegiac *topoi* and themes throughout the *Art of Love*. The didactic *magister amoris* offers an unemotional account of this event in which the feelings of the elegiac poet-lover have been removed. So, the tone of passionate remorse that infuses the *Loves* version of this episode gives way to a cooler tone of dispassionate observation and commentary, with the realisation that the lover's mistress has manipulated this 'fight' to her own advantage. The *Art of Love* then offers a new perspective into the world of the elegiac lover, transforming erotic failure and frustration into triumph and success, and elegiac tradition into didactic sermon. Certainly, the *Loves* presented a witty and far from serious view of love, but its playful humour engaged our sympathy with the poet-lover who, according to the rules of elegiac love, always loses at this game. The didactic *Art of Love* also treats love as a game, but unlike the *Loves*, it treats love as a game to be played seriously: the lover of the *Art of Love* plays to win.

Although many readers have been struck by the manipulative cynicism of much of the instructions detailed in the *Art of Love*, some modern readers have been favourably impressed by the emphasis upon sexual equality that appears to play an important role in the poem's teachings. This is a contentious issue in Ovidian scholarship, dividing readings and readers into those who characterise the poet and his poems as sympathetic to women, and those who see his love songs as sexist and even misogynist. Some readers maintain that Ovid's literary objectification of women is 'akin to pornography', some claim that Ovid possessed 'an intuitive understanding of female psychology', while others suggest that he was 'an early advocate of women's rights and gender equality'. One critic even suggests that 'Ovid actually liked women as a sex – something that cannot be taken for granted in the case of many other Latin poets'! The *Art of Love* offers evidence to support each of these opposing views. It is true that, having offered two books teaching men how to seduce women, Ovid redresses this gender imbalance with the addition of a third book teaching women how to seduce men (3.1-6):

> I have armed the Greeks against the Amazons; but there are
> > weapons
> > Which I must give to you, Penthesilea, and to your troops.
> Go into battle as equals; the winners will be those who are
> > supported by
> > Loving Venus and the boy who flies over the whole world.
> It is not fair that naked and defenceless girls should fight with
> > armed men.
> > Such a victory would be embarrassing to you men.

But this third book is clearly not directed towards an exclusively female audience (notice that line six directly addresses a male audience), and even in the characterisation of his female pupils as Amazons – mythical female warriors renowned not simply for their battles against Greek heroes but for their legendary defeats at the hands of Greek men – Ovid betrays both his true sympathies and his female readers.

In the first two books aimed at a male audience, Ovid maintains that both women and men enjoy sex equally. He instructs his male pupils to make love to a woman slowly, aiming for both partners to orgasm together (2.717-32). He even claims that the mutual pleasure of sex and particularly the satisfaction of mutual orgasm are the reasons why he personally prefers to have sex with women rather then men (2.683f):

> I hate any sex in which both partners do not melt.
> That's why a boy's love appeals to me so little.

But in Book 3 (3.797f; 801-3), this view of the mutual pleasures of heterosexual love is undermined by Ovid's advice to his female readers on how to fake an orgasm:

> But you to whom nature denies the pleasure of sex,
>   Fake enjoyment with deceiving sounds.
> Only, when you fake it, make sure that you aren't caught:
>   Make it look convincing with your movements and with
>   your eyes.
> Let your words and panting breath make your orgasm clear.

What becomes clear from these instructions is the supreme importance of a man's sexual pleasure. Ovid stresses that a woman's orgasm contributes much to a man's enjoyment of sex and it is this notion perhaps, rather than any proto-feminist idea of sexual equality or mutual enjoyment of sex, that directs his advice here. Similarly, Ovid's insistence throughout the *Art of Love* that women actually enjoy sex should not be seen as a particularly forward-looking view of sexual equality or one that anticipates modern attitudes to female sexuality. The assertion that women enjoy sex as much as and even more than men underpins Ovid's teachings in the arts of love. He reassures his male pupils that women are, by 'nature', creatures with high libidos and that all women desire to be seduced and loved. And if women desire sex too, then men need have no fear that their sexual advances – if properly made – will be rejected (1.269f; 277-80):

> First be assured in your own minds that all women can be
> caught;
> You only have to spread out your nets to catch them.
>
> If it did not suit us men to ask the women first,
> The women, already won over, would do the asking.
> In soft meadows the heifer moos to the bull;
> The mare always whinnies to the hard-hoofed stallion.

This farmyard image of female desire is hardly flattering to women but is designed to give encouragement to Ovid's insecure male pupils. To further illustrate his point that women are naturally more lustful than men, and only restrained by cultural convention from making the first move, Ovid reminds his readers of a few aptly chosen classical myths concerning excessively 'passionate' women – among them, the infamous Clytemnestra, who conspired with her lover to butcher her husband; Medea, who murdered her lover's new wife and her own children; Byblis, who fell in love with her brother; Myrrha, who seduced her own father; Phaedra, who fell in love with her stepson; and Pasiphaë, wife of Minos and mother to the monstrous minotaur, conceived from her bestial affair with a bull (1.283-342). Ovid tells the shocking story of Pasiphaë and the bull at some length, infusing his salacious narrative with characteristic humour, as effectively reproduced in Peter Jones' translation for *Forum Magazine*:

53

Pasiphaë, wife of king Minos of Crete, fell in love with a bull! She mooned after it in the fields all day, picking it leaves and lush grass, looking daggers at the heifers and thinking, 'What on earth can he see in that old cow – thinks she's a real raver, no doubt': and promptly ordering it off to the altar to be sacrificed ('And how do you like her now, huh?'). You can see how female lust far outstrips ours.

Although Ovid presents this story of unbridled female lust in a light-hearted, comedic way, more troubling for the modern reader is the way in which this view of female sexuality appears to shape Ovid's attitude towards violence and rape in the *Art of Love*. In Book 3, he warns his female readers not to get drunk at parties or to fall asleep after dinner, for to do so is to run the risk of rape and assault (3.765f). His evident lack of sympathy for any woman who finds herself in this situation is striking:

> A woman lying soaked with too much wine is an ugly thing;
>   She deserves to suffer whatever she gets.

In Book 1, Ovid assures his male readers that women 'really' enjoy rape, advising his pupils that 'You are allowed to use force; women like it' – and supporting this provocative claim by giving an account of mythical heroines who have been raped and subsequently fallen in love with their rapists (1.664-708). His list of mythological *exempla* is not long, but he demonstrates the validity of his lesson by telling the story of Achilles and Deidamia. At the start of the Trojan war, fearing for her son's life, Achilles' mother had disguised her teenage son as a girl and sent him to live among the women (1.697-700):

> But by chance, the royal princess shared the same bedroom;
>   By her rape, she discovered that he was a man.

54

> By force she was taken, so we must believe;
> But by force she wanted to be taken anyway.

The light-hearted and often frivolous treatment of sex in the *Art of Love* seems refreshing and 'modern', but Ovid's light-hearted and frivolous treatment of rape raises serious questions for twenty-first-century readers of the poem. Perhaps Ovid is being serious when he claims that women secretly enjoy rape. Perhaps he is being deliberately – and dangerously – provocative. But before we condemn Ovid as a misogynist, we should remember that nothing in the *Art of Love* is straightforward, that the role of expert *praeceptor amoris* is precisely a part that Ovid the poet plays in this poem. A useful twenty-first-century corollary could be made with the rap musician Eminem. Marshall Mathers has many rap *personae*, and his rap alter-ego Slim Shady has been charged with inciting violence against women through misogynist lyrics. His defenders (including feminist Germaine Greer) point out that the artist should not be confused with his artistic *personae*, and suggest that Eminem's aggressive and misogynist lyrics expose the pervasive misogyny that has come to characterise American rap and hip-hop. Defenders of Ovid might also point out, then, that Ovid's explicit and sometimes exaggerated treatments of elegiac tropes – particularly *servitium* and *militia amoris* – expose the pervasive motif of sexual violence in the world of Latin love elegy. And they might also argue that the attitudes to women and rape expressed in the *Art of Love* belong to Ovid's poetic alter-ego, the *praeceptor amoris*, and not necessarily to the poet himself.

In fact, Ovid himself tried to use this same argument to defend charges of the poem's (and the poet's) perceived immorality and indecency – but without success. For, read against the background of Augustus' political programmes of social and moral reform at this time, Ovid's erotic writings were seen to pose a real (or perhaps a 'real') challenge to the sexual politics of their day. Crucially for Ovid, new legislation passed in 18 BC now made adultery a criminal rather than a civil offence – punishable by the full authority of Roman law. And, in Book 3 of the *Art of Love*, Ovid explicitly teaches girls how to deceive their guardians – that is, their fathers or husbands. Nor does Ovid pretend to be ignorant of the new laws promoting decent family values and criminalizing adultery. He writes (3.611-14):

> How it is possible to deceive a crafty husband,
>> Or a watchful guardian, I was going to skip over.
> A bride should fear her husband: A guard set over a bride should
>>> be secure.
>> This is only right, and the laws, justice, and honour order it.

But he does *not* skip over this section. Instead, with the now familiar excuse that he is teaching courtesans how to deceive their guardians and lovers rather than wives how to cheat on their husbands, he immediately goes on to advise his female readers to write secret letters to their lovers in the bath, using milk instead of ink to avoid detection – or even writing directly onto the back of a slave girl and sending her to a lover in place of a note. He suggests that a careful 'guardian' can do nothing to stop a girl meeting her lover when she goes to the theatre or to the races, or to the baths or to the temple of Isis. He recommends visiting a 'sick' friend and taking advantage of both the situation and the friend's bed to entertain a lover. And if none of these tricks work, he proposes that a girl can always get her guardian drunk or even drug him so as to slip out to a secret rendezvous. Helpful tips such as these were more than enough to convince Augustus that Ovid had overstepped the mark this time. The poet was charged as 'a professor of foul adultery' – *obsceni doctor adulterii* – and banished from Rome, his poems banned from public performance and circulation. Ovid's playful poetry had landed him in serious trouble.

3

The Heroines' Letters

PLAYER: Tragedy, sir. Deaths and disclosures, universal and particular, dénouements both unexpected and inexorable, transvestite melodrama on all levels including the suggestive. We transport you into a world of intrigue and illusion ... clowns, if you like, murderers – we can do you ghosts and battles, on the skirmish level, heroes, villains, tormented lovers – set pieces in the poetic vein; we can do you rapiers or rape or both, by all means, faithless wives and ravished virgins – flagrante delicto at a price, but that comes under realism for which there are special terms.

Tom Stoppard, *Rosencrantz and Guildenstern are Dead*

In writing the *Loves* and *Art of Love*, Ovid had revolutionised the world of elegy, playfully experimenting with every character and characteristic of the elegiac tradition until they – and the short-lived genre of Roman love elegy itself – were exhausted. In the meantime, fresh resources were needed for his next poetic project and, in the *Heroides*, or *Heroines' Letters*, Ovid looked to the world of myth to provide him with new material and a new approach to love elegy. In the *Heroines' Letters*, his next experiment, Ovid came up with his most innovative work – a collection of poetic letters or verse epistles.

Ovid's innovation in the *Heroines' Letters* is to take a series of well-known myths and legends and to offer us the 'other' side of the story. Just as Tom Stoppard's play *Rosencrantz and Guildenstern are Dead* offers us a new look at Shakespeare's *Hamlet* 'from the wings', or as the sitcom *Frasier* allows us to follow the life of a character after his role in another work (*Cheers*) has ended, so the *Heroines' Letters* retell familiar stories from the perspectives of marginal characters. Each letter allows a minor female figure from a popular work of classical literature to take centre stage for a moment and to tell us her story in her own words. Women from myth, tragedy, and epic – united by a common literary bond that even allows the poet Sappho her place – are transformed into elegiac lovers, lamenting the hard hearts and infidelities of the men who have deserted them.

Perhaps the most ingenious aspect of the *Heroines' Letters* is the way in which Ovid subverts his readers' literary expectations. Not only does he play with our expectations of the proper form and content of an elegiac poem, but he also challenges accepted popular conceptions of his mythological and literary heroines. So, not only is the Lesbian Sappho 'set straight' here, and presented writing her letter to a male lover, Phaon, but some of the traditionally blameless and sympathetic female figures of classical literature, such as the faithful Penelope and the naïve Ariadne, are seen in the *Heroines' Letters* in a new and often unsympathetic light – as manipulative and scheming, unreasonable and stroppy. On the other hand, some of the least sympathetic women of literary history, such as the evil Medea, witch and child-killer, and lustful Phaedra, who falsely accused her stepson of rape, are presented in the *Heroines' Letters* as sensitive and sympathetic characters, deserving of our compassion and empathy.

Ovid's first heroine, Penelope – Homer's legendary paragon of virtue and patience and a role-model for women in the ancient world – appears here as a role-model for Ovid's transformation of literary heroines into elegiac *puellae*. Ovid expects his readers to be already familiar with Homer's heroine from the *Odyssey*, but the Penelope that he presents as the writer of his first *Heroines' Letters* is a very different woman. In Homer, Penelope is like her heroic husband Odysseus: intelligent, patient, and crafty, unpicking by night the shroud that she weaves by day so as to distract and delay the attentions of the suitors who would marry her and usurp Odysseus' place. In the *Heroines' Letters*, she is also like her husband, but here her character is not simply intelligent, patient, and crafty, but cunning, long-suffering, and suspicious. And, Ovid boldly hints, even unfaithful.

Her letter is full of sexual puns and *double-entendres*, which challenge the stereotypical and idealised image of Penelope as a virtuous and faithful wife. The erotic subtext to her letter could be read as a reflection of the sexual frustration of a *puella* who has become an unattractive old woman during the twenty years that her husband has been away – as Penelope herself suggests (1.115f). Indeed, some critics have described her as a sex-starved and sex-obsessed old woman. Alternatively, the sexual innuendo might be seen to hint at another side to Penelope the legendary paradigm of wifely virtue. In *Loves* 1.8, Ovid had already tarnished Penelope's reputation by intimating that when she famously tested the suitors with Odysseus' mighty bow – promising to marry the man who was strong enough to string it – she was actually testing their sexual prowess (1.8.47f):

> When Penelope was testing the virility of those young men with
> the bow,
> Horny (*corneus*) was the bow that proved their potency.

Here Ovid uses the Latin *corneus* – a popular synonym for penis – to make his somewhat less than subtle corny sexual pun. In *Heroines' Letters* 1, he is similarly suggestive, describing the suitors in erotically charged language as a 'lustful crowd' who 'press against' or even 'press into' Penelope (1.88), and who, in Ulysses' absence, 'plunder' and pillage his possessions – including his wife's 'body' (1.90). Chaste Penelope, Ovid hints, may not have held out against all those suitors, resisting their sexual advances and offers of marriage, quite as virtuously or as successfully as literary history tells us.

In these new guises, Ovid's heroines also rewrite some of the minor yet momentous details of literary history. Ovid's Dido, radically challenging Virgil's canonical account of her affair with Aeneas, claims to be pregnant with Aeneas' child when he leaves her in order to found the future city of Rome. She also alleges that, as a serial heartbreaker, he cruelly left his first wife Creusa too, selfishly abandoning her to die in the burning city when he fled from Troy. Other heroines reveal in their letters that, contrary to popular misconception and literary misrepresentation, they played daring and active roles in aiding their heroic lovers, and without their support many of these famous heroes would have failed in their heroic quests. In this respect, the *Heroines' Letters* develops the elegiac practice of subverting conventional gender roles to an extreme. The traditional persona of the elegiac male poet-lover (who plays a feminised and submissive role in relation to his mistress or *domina*) is now transformed into the persona of an elegiac female writer-lover. This 'gender-bending' is the key to appreciating the *Heroines' Letters*. It allows Ovid to explore not only the other side of some of the most famous love stories in classical history, but also the other side of the elegiac love affair. Although his predecessor Propertius had attempted to offer some poetic insights into the world of Roman erotic elegy from the imagined perspective of his mistress, Cynthia, Ovid's is the first sustained experiment in representing a woman's experience of the elegiac sphere.

The elegiac language and elegiac tropes that recur throughout the *Heroines' Letters* serve to highlight this role reversal. In Roman love elegy, women are hard-hearted, unfaithful, manipulative, mercenary, and deceitful, while men are their devoted, deceived, misused, and lovesick slaves. In the *Heroines' Letters*, these roles are reversed. The heroines still refer to themselves as *puellae* and as *dominae*, but now it is the women who are the lovesick slaves, used and abused by their lovers, and it is now the men who are cruel and faithless. Faithful Penelope waits for Ulysses to make his slow way back from Troy, suspecting (rightly) that he has had affairs with other women during his long absence. Dido, 'inflamed' with passion, 'wounded' and driven 'crazy' by her love for Aeneas, wonders how the son of Venus and brother to Cupid could show so little respect for Love and for her. The poet Sappho laments that although her poetry is famed for its power to move others, the cold hard heart of her lover Phaon remains untouched by her words of love. In fact, looked at as a whole, the *Heroines' Letters* provides a remarkably broad range of different patterns and configurations of *amor*. In the *Heroines' Letters* Ovid drives the elegiac genre into brand new territory, using elegy as the medium for love songs about the complicated love that can exist between wife and husband, sister and brother, daughter and mother, daughter and father, stepmother and stepson – each relationship and each mode of *amor* expressed and explored in terms of the elegiac lover's discourse.

Elegiac motifs also reappear in the elegiac 'mirror' world of the *Heroines' Letters*. Penelope describes how the men who returned from Troy had told her stories of the war, illustrating their tales with images drawn in wine on the table (1.31-6) – an epic variation of a familiar elegiac mode of sign-language used between lovers at dinner parties. Phyllis complains that she trusted the unfaithful Demophoön (2.49-54), believing his false promises, his solemn oaths sworn by the gods, and his sad tears, which she now suspects were fake – a trick taught by Ovid himself in the *Art of*

Love. Briseis sees herself literally and figuratively as enslaved to Achilles – representing herself as a 'slave to love' caught in the same bonds of *servitium amoris* that we see in Ovid's *Loves*. Oenone is concerned that the letter she writes to Paris will not be read by him, because his wife will forbid him to read it or else intercept it – an everyday fear for the elegiac lover, who worries that his girlfriend's husband or guardian may intercept his love letters. And Hypsipyle believes that Jason has been bewitched by another woman – appropriately in this case, the witch Medea – accusing Medea of practising precisely the kind of love-magic described in *Loves* 1.8 and 2.1.

Alongside his elegiac writing, Ovid's early rhetorical training can also be seen to exert an influence upon the style and tone of the *Heroines' Letters*. One of the principal exercises taught and practised in Roman schools of rhetoric was that of speaking in character or *ethopoeia*, in which the speaker produced an imaginary speech appropriate to a famous historical or mythological character at a significant moment in their lives. So, students might be required to imagine themselves in the position of Medea at the point of murdering her children, or of Sulla at the point of his abdication. The parallels with Ovid's *Heroines' Letters* are clear and some scholars have interpreted this collection of verse letters as a mere compilation of such rhetorical exercises, lacking in any real artistic merit. But such readings emphasise the rhetorical characteristics of the *Heroines' Letters* at the expense of their other literary features and influences. For, while the rhetorical conventions of the *ethopoeia* play an important role in shaping the heroines' letters, other literary and dramatic forms also make a significant contribution to their style and form.

Perhaps most obviously, given the extent to which Ovid draws from Greek tragedy as a source for this work, the *Heroines' Letters* shares much with the classical tradition of the dramatic monologue. Parallels can be drawn, in particular, between the letters of Ovid's heroines and the monologues delivered by Euripides' tragic women, and a number of Euripides' tragic heroines are used as direct models for Ovid's own heroines – including Phaedra, Hypsipyle, Medea, and Laodamia. Yet, Ovid also draws from Greek and Roman epic to shape his heroines and the set-piece speeches given to characters such as Penelope in the *Odyssey* and Dido in the *Aeneid* similarly leave a mark on Ovid's poetry here. It might even be suggested that the heroines' letters are, at some level, Ovid's own letters to his literary predecessors: written to Homer and Euripides, Catullus and Virgil, commenting upon and critiquing their works, and asking questions about their representations of women and their stories of love and lovers.

The epistolarity of the *Heroines' Letters*, and the significance of the poems' form as poetic *letters* has often been overlooked by readers and critics, dismissed as little more than a literary gimmick or conceit. But recent scholarship focusing upon the epistolarity of the collection has raised some intriguing questions about the intended addressees and readers of Ovid's *Heroines' Letters*. As Joe Farrell has pointed out, the letters 'present themselves quite clearly as love letters from Penelope to Ulysses, from Briseis to Achilles, and so on', but it is not clear how we as readers fit into this correspondence between letter writer and addressee. The letters are explicitly not addressed to us, but we read them anyway. Are we then supposed to imagine ourselves as Ulysses, Achilles, et al., reading the *Heroines' Letters* as if we were the men to whom they are written and addressed? Perhaps. But the heroines frequently write of their fears that their letters will never reach their intended destination and their intended readers, that their letters will be deliberately intercepted or fall into the hands of the wrong readers. Are we then to imagine ourselves as the unsympathetic readers who have accidentally or wrongfully intercepted these love letters?

Oenone's letter to Paris (5) makes this possibility explicit in her opening line 'Will you read this to the end? Or will your new wife forbid it?' Oenone's fear that Helen will intercept or forbid Paris to read her letter allows us as readers to imagine ourselves reading it as if we were either Paris *or* Helen. In her letter to Ulysses, Penelope writes that she uses passing sailors as putative 'postmen', hoping that one of them may meet with Ulysses somewhere and someday (1.59-62):

> Whoever turns his voyaging ship towards these shores,
> Leaves only when I have asked him a hundred questions
> about you,
> And so that he can deliver it to you, if he should see you
> anywhere,
> I give him a letter, written in my own hand.

As readers of this letter, we may imagine ourselves as one of these sailors, casually or unscrupulously reading that which was intended for the eyes of another. Yet, Duncan Kennedy has shown that if we read the intertextual clues contained in Penelope's letter to Ulysses carefully enough, we will realise that the anonymous sailor to whom she intends to entrust this letter is in fact Ulysses himself – according to Homer's *Odyssey*, only recently returned home to Ithaca and still in disguise, unrecognised by his wife or family. In this case, then, we may assume that Ovid intends us to read Penelope's letter as if we were the man to whom it is addressed – Ulysses himself. Critics and readers have noticed, though, that other letters appear to be addressed to more than one person. Hermione's letter to Orestes (8) also speaks directly to her mother, Hypsipyle's letter to Jason (6) seems also to be addressed to her rival Medea, and Canace's letter to Macareus (11) is addressed to her brother, but has just as much to say to their father. The role assigned to us as readers of all these letters is not simply that of snoop or voyeur, then. The direct and intimate exchange of love letter between its writer and addressee is compromised and complicated in each of the *Heroines' Letters*, allowing for – and even inviting – different readings and different responses.

Appropriately, perhaps, Ovid's verse letters have received mixed reviews from readers and critics. Grant Showerman, writing 'in appreciation of the *Heroides*', offers the type of qualified praise that has become commonplace in critical evaluations of the *Heroines' Letters*. He claims that:

> The *Heroides* are not a work of the highest order of genius. Their language, nearly always artificial, frequently rhetorical, and often diffuse, is the same throughout – whether from the lips of barbarian Medea or Sappho the poetess. The heroines and heroes who speak it are creatures from the world of legend, are not always warm flesh and blood, and rarely communicate their passion to us.

We might wonder what he would have said 'in criticism of the *Heroides*', given this harsh assessment of the letters' rhetoricity and monotony. But Showerman is not alone in his appreciation of the poem *despite* its perceived flaws rather than *because* of its merits. L.P. Wilkinson, whose project to rescue Ovid's literary reputation in *Ovid Recalled* heralded the dawn of a modern renaissance in Ovidian studies, similarly damns the *Heroines' Letters* with faint praise. He describes the work as a stodgy 'plum pudding', declaring that 'the first slice is appetising enough, but each further slice becomes colder and less digestible'.

Such charges that the *Heroides* are boring and monotonous, particularly when read one after another, continued well into the 1990s when a new trend emerged, denying that the repetitions of character and theme in the epistles were monotonous, and declaring instead that they demonstrated a virtuoso performance in variation. New readings of the *Heroines' Letters* show that in recycling familiar elegiac tropes and conceits in each of his verse epistles, Ovid not only reshapes them, but also puts them to new uses. So, in her letter to Orestes (8), Hermione complains about her hard-hearted lover and his ill treatment of her in a style with which Ovid's readers have now become familiar. Yet, closer reading of her letter reveals that Hermione's typical elegiac complaints are directed more towards her mother (the infamous Helen of Troy) than her lover. Telling the untold story of a daughter left behind when her mother takes a lover and runs away with him to Troy, Hermione writes of the pain of abandonment, rejection, and heartbreak from the perspective of a child. The same elegiac features of lament and complaint that we have already seen in the *Loves* and the preceding *Heroines' Letters* are seen in an entirely new light here. With a poignancy that is only enhanced by the familiarity of situation and emotion, Hermione writes about her memories of the day on which her mother left for Troy (8.75f; 79f; 91f):

> I hardly remember it really, and yet I do remember it.
>> Everywhere there was grief, everywhere anxiety and fear.
>
> I myself, tearing out my hair – not so very long back then – kept
>> shouting:
>> 'Mother! Will you go away without me? Without me?'
>
> You were not here in my early years, my mother, to catch
>> The loving words from the tripping tongue of a little girl
>>> (*puella*).

Remembering herself as a small child, Hermione casts herself in the role of a rejected elegiac *puella*, in much the same way that all the other heroines of Ovid's letters style themselves. Like the other heroines, Hermione grieves and protests at her cruel treatment, but here she is a *puella* who has been abandoned and rejected by her mother rather than an unfaithful lover, offering a striking variation on the elegiac themes of love and loss that resonate throughout the other *Heroines' Letters*.

It is for characteristics such as this that John Dryden famously regarded the *Heroines' Letters* as Ovid's 'most perfect piece' of poetry, but he too saw imperfections in the collection. In the preface to his own English translation of the *Heroines' Letters*, he suggests that Ovid's heroines are not altogether plausible as legendary lovers:

> Perhaps he has Romanized his Grecian dames too much, and made them speak sometimes as if they had been born in the city of Rome, and under the empire of Augustus.

Dryden also observes dryly that 'Ovid's heroines are not too miserable to make puns' and that they often 'speak more eloquently than the violence of their passion would admit'. And it is these same flaws in the characters of Ovid's heroines that continue to cause concern for some modern readers of the *Heroines' Letters*. Critics of the collection particularly find fault with the poems for their artificiality and lack of 'realism'. One such critic wonders where Ariadne managed to find writing materials on the uninhabited island of Naxos. Another wonders how she intended to send her letter to Theseus in Athens, suggesting that the postal service from the deserted island of Naxos cannot have been very reliable. Yet another complains that Briseis lived in a primitive, pre-literate society and should not have been able to write at all – although admittedly, she does say in her letter that her 'barbarian hand' finds it difficult to write in Greek.

While these complaints are hard to take seriously, criticisms that Ovid's characteristic wit intrudes too often into the heroines' letters – that he is, in Dryden's words, 'frequently witty out of season' – are less easy to dismiss. When Ariadne, abandoned by Theseus, tears out her hair in passionate grief in *Heroines' Letters* 10 and begs her heartless lover to come back for her, her emotional speech is sabotaged by Ovid's cruel sense of humour (10.145-7).

These hands, worn out with beating at my heartbroken chest,
 I stretch out to you across the wide sea, in misery.
My hair – what's left of it anyway – I hold out to you in despair.

Ariadne, it seems, has literally been tearing her hair out, and now waves 'what's left of it' to Theseus as his ship sails away – a disturbing and blackly comic image that is reminiscent of *Loves* 1.14.

Similar ironies and incongruities pervade Briseis' letter, which offers an excellent case study through which to examine some of Ovid's best and worst characteristics in the *Heroines' Letters*. In the first few lines of her letter Briseis apologises for her poor handwriting and questions her right to write words of complaint or *querela* – that is, her right to write elegiac verse (3.1-8):

The writing which you read comes from the stolen Briseis,
 Poorly scribbled in Greek by her barbarian hand.
Whatever blots you see her tears have made,
 But tears too have the weight of words.
If it is right for me to complain a little about you, my master and
              my husband,
 I will complain about you, my master and my husband.
That I was handed over so swiftly when the king asked,
 That is not your fault – although, this too is your fault;

3. The Heroines' Letters

It is ironic of course that the epistle Briseis writes in the *Heroines' Letters* comes to us written in Latin and not in Greek, and the 'copy' of her letter that we have bears no traces of the blots of her tears. The opening lines of the epistle remind us that we do not have the 'original' love letter from Briseis to Achilles in our hands – and that here we do not have the 'original' Briseis. Her writing appears to us in a 'translation' and in a form now free of the tearstains that marred the imagined 'original' work. Ovid, it seems, has edited her letter and the heroine herself.

Briseis' letter to Achilles is often regarded as Ovid's attempt to produce an elegiac reworking of the *Iliad*, and it is clear that this poem draws much of its material directly from Books 1-19 of Homer's epic – including Achilles' repeated threats to leave Troy and return home, the visit of Agamemnon's envoys to persuade him to stay, and Briseis' lament over the corpse of Achilles' beloved Patroclus. Yet, Ovid's version of these incidents does not offer us a simple adaptation of Homer's story or character. Rather, his revision of the *Iliad* through the eyes of Briseis, a minor and marginal female figure in the *Iliad*, provides us with an elegiac commentary on the world of Homeric epic. Ovid's Briseis was first an epic heroine and Homer's representation of Briseis' lament in the *Iliad* (19.282-300) clearly provides the basic material from which Ovid's elegiac heroine is constructed. In Homer's account of the embassy to Achilles in *Iliad* 9, he catalogues the expensive gifts promised by Agamemnon to Achilles if he will stay in Troy. Included with the gold, the bronze vessels, and the prize-winning horses are 'seven women from Lesbos, skilled in weaving' (9.270f) and Achilles' pick of the king's daughters. In Briseis' account of the same embassy in *Heroides* 3, she too lists the costly gifts that Agamemnon has promised to send to compensate and appease Achilles, and she chides her lover for refusing to accept such a profitable deal. But she also points out that he can have no need for

any of the women Agamemnon has offered – jealously, begrudg-
ingly, and comically adding to her list (3.26-38):

> Go now, call yourself an eager lover!
> They came to you, the sons of Telemon and Amyntor –
> One closer in terms of blood-ties, one a comrade –
> And Odysseus, through whom I was to be ransomed, together
> > with
> Rich gifts to support their entreating prayers:
> Twenty gleaming vessels of wrought bronze,
> And seven tripods, equal in weight and craftmanship;
> Added to these were two lots of five gold talents,
> Two lots of six horses guaranteed always to win,
> And (what there was no need of) girls of outstanding beauty,
> Lesbian girls taken when their home was overthrown,
> And together with all of this (although you had no need of a
> > bride)
> A bride – any one of Agamemnon's three girls.

Here, like a scheming and mercenary *puella* from the world of
elegy, Ovid's Briseis displays a calculating and astute appreciation
of her own value. But she also reveals in her (mis)quotation of
Homer the way in which women are so often reduced to the status
of objects in the world of epic – bartered and exchanged between
men as brides or as prizes of war.

Taken away from her husband and family together with their
other possessions as Achilles' war prize, taken away from Achilles
by Agamemnon to compensate the king for the loss of another
girl, and offered back to Achilles in exchange for his return to the
battlefield, Briseis is repeatedly bartered and exchanged between
different men – an object of value, but an object nonetheless. Yet,
ironically, in being carried across from the world of the *Iliad* to
the *Heroines' Letters*, Ovid's Briseis has once again been

exchanged between two men. She has been passed from one literary camp to another: passed from Homer to Ovid, from the Greek to the Roman, from the epicist to the elegist, a pawn exchanged between two male poets – just as she was once exchanged between Achilles and Agamemnon. But in the elegiac world of the *Heroines' Letters*, Briseis reminds us that she is and always was far more than a mere pawn in the power games played out between these men. Recalling the principal theme of Homer's epic *Iliad* – the wrath of Achilles – Briseis reminds us that *she* was the cause of that anger (3.89). Because of her Achilles and Agamemnon quarrelled, because of her Achilles withdrew himself and his troops from the war, because of her Patroclus fought and died in his place, and because of her the Trojan War was decided as Homer tells it. If Homer's Briseis seemed only a minor player in the drama of the Trojan War, Ovid's Briseis exposes the major role that she 'really' played.

But Briseis' letter does not only expose some of the hidden aspects of Homer's *Iliad*. In identifying herself in her epistle as the 'captive Briseis' who has been 'enslaved' by Achilles, Briseis exposes through a process of *reductio ad absurdum* one of the banner tropes of Latin love elegy – *servitium amoris* – the metaphorical configuration of love as a form of slavery, and the lover as a 'slave' both to love and to his 'mistress'. This popular trope in elegiac love poetry is made redundant by Briseis' relationship to Achilles' in the *Heroines' Letters*, however: she is *literally* both his lover and his slave. Achilles is not just metaphorically her master or *dominus*, he is really her master and she his slave; it is no elegiac lover's exaggeration to claim that her life and death are in his hands (3.140f). It is this status as Achilles' slave that renders Briseis' allusions to the familiar elegiac representation of lover and beloved as master or mistress and slave both funny and pathetic (3.75-82):

Me, I shall be your lowly slave and spin out the task given me,
  And the full distaff will grow less with my threading.
Only, do not let your wife – I pray – be mean to me.
  I do not know why, but she may be unfair in some way.
Do not let her tear my hair in your presence
  While you say lightly: 'She too was once mine'.
Or let her, but only if I am not left behind in contempt.
  Ah this is the fear that shakes me – poor me – to my bones!

Although Briseis seems to recognise the potential hardships of the life of a female slave – particularly the life of a slave with a mistress such as Ovid's Corinna, as stereotyped in the *Loves* – she nevertheless seeks to persuade us that she would be amenable to such a life, if only she might be permitted to live with the man that she loves. Yet, this willing acceptance of both *servitium amoris* and literal servitude on Briseis' part may also be viewed as a strategic ploy designed to win over, to 'capture' and 'dominate' her lover. The pose of subservience adopted by the poet-lover of the *Loves* and *Art of Love* has been identified and exposed as a strategy of 'masculine assertiveness' by some critics, and we might be tempted to view Briseis' pose of subservience in the *Heroines' Letters* in the same way.

   In her opening address to Achilles, Briseis plays with the ambiguous nature of her relationship with her captor, lover, and master, confusing the status of their relationship. Briseis then continues to manipulate this ambiguity to her advantage, reminding Achilles of the rights that are due to her because of her status as his slave, as well as those that are appropriate to her status as his mistress. Her final words repeat a pattern that is worked throughout her letter – a forceful imperative *ordering* Achilles to use his authority as her master to *tell* her to come to him (3.150-4):

What you gave as a victor to foe, I ask as a lover.
Those whom it would be better for you to destroy, Neptune's
    Troy offers as subjects for your sword. Go seek the enemy.
Only, whether you prepare to drive your ships with oars
    Or to stay – by your authority as my master, tell me to
                      come!

And, crucially, from our foreknowledge of the events of the *Iliad*, we know that Achilles will stay in Troy, that he will bid Briseis to come back, and that the lovers will be reunited – because all of this has already happened. In the final book of the *Iliad* and the last scene in which we see Achilles, the two are shown sleeping peacefully together in Achilles' tent (*Iliad* 24.765f), lovers always already reunited.

4

The Calendar

I love, I love, I love my calendar girl
Yeah, sweet calendar girl
I love, I love, I love my calendar girl
Each and every day of the year

(January) you start the year off fine
(February) you're my little valentine
(March) I'm gonna march you down the aisle
(April) you're the easter bunny when you smile

Yeah, yeah, my heart's in a whirl
I love, I love, I love my little calendar girl.

Neil Sedaka, 'Calendar Girl'

In 2003, Hollywood celebrated the 'real life' story of twelve unlikely heroines with the movie *Calendar Girls*. Twelve members of the Rydale Women's Institute gave their annual charity calendar a provocative new look, and behind the traditional photographs of jams, cakes, and artfully arranged flowers, each month featured a WI member – nude. But calendars featuring erotic – and incongruous – images, giving a playful and sexy twist to tradition, are nothing new. Ovid's *Fasti* – a playful mix of tradition and sex – had given the Roman calendar a provocative new look two thousand years earlier.

The poem begins with the first day of January and follows an ordered chronological pattern until the last day of June, where it ends – interrupted, so Ovid claims in the *Sad Songs* (2.549ff), by his banishment to Tomis. Critics have generally accepted this claim as an uncomplicated statement of fact, attributing the loss of the second half of the poem to various causes. It is often assumed that the poet grew bored of his ambitious undertaking at the halfway stage, or that the creative pressure of simultaneous work upon the *Metamorphoses* and the *Calendar* proved too great. J.G. Frazer (whose *Golden Bough* is indebted to Ovid's *Calendar*) famously suggested that the last six books were lost – 'possibly in the post, which can hardly have been very regular or secure at Tomi'. Such views, however, must necessarily remain speculative. We know very little about the fate of the last six books. They seem to have 'disappeared' without trace. But it is possible that they were never written in the first place. It is possible (and probable) that Ovid planned to conclude his calendar with the sixth month – without treating the politically charged months of July and August, which honoured (of course) the emperors *Julius* and *Augustus* Caesar.

In the *Art of Love*, Ovid had already treated the subject of sex and timing, teaching his readers the best times of the year to pick up girls – and the times when women are best avoided. He had also directed a less than subtle attack upon Augustus' political 'back to basics' campaign which aimed to promote traditional and wholesome family values – even going so far as to recommend the buildings and monuments featured in Augustus' ambitious public building programme as ideal places to pick up women or for lovers to meet. In the *Calendar*, he takes a new approach to 'dates' and 'dating', reworking the elegiac conceits of the *Art of Love* and again probing Augustus' programmes for social and moral reform.

Ovid's *Calendar* deals with three key elements as it moves through the course of the Roman year – history, astronomy, and religion: Ovid's equivalents to the *Calendar Girls'* jams, cakes, and flowers. And like the *Calendar Girls'* props, these traditional features are carefully positioned so as to provide respectable cover for the 'naughtier' bits of his poem. The historical element concerns the retelling and re-presentation of many of Rome's myths and legends in relation to particular calendar dates. So, the traditional date of 24 February given to the expulsion of the kings of Rome grants Ovid the occasion to tell the story of the rape of Lucretia and its consequences for Rome's last king, Tarquin the Proud.

The measured movements of constellations through the night sky were employed as precise markers in ancient calendar systems, including the one used in Rome, offering Ovid legitimate reason to record the seasonal appearances of such familiar constellations as Cancer, Capricorn, and Aquarius in his *Calendar*. But Ovid is no astrologer. He regularly gets it wrong, attributing false dates for the rising and setting of very many of the stars and constellations that he records. In one case, he even identifies a fictitious constellation, the Kite (3.793ff), apparently interpreting the reference in a Greek calendar to the arrival of the first kite of spring as an astronomical rather than an ornithological event. But for Ovid, it seems, the rising or setting of a star is significant only in so far as it may be used as a prop or prompt for the narration of an appropriate myth. So, on 11 February, the appearance of the star Boötes in the constellation of the Bear (2.153ff) gives rise to the story of Callisto, her rape by Jupiter, her metamorphosis into a bear, and her subsequent apotheosis.

The religious element of the *Calendar* incorporates aetiological explanations for the many festivals and rituals recorded by the Roman calendar, making a significant contribution to our knowledge of Roman religion – for which detailed and reliable sources of evidence are rare. Although Ovid's inconsistent and ambiguous explanations for many of the festivals he describes may occasionally frustrate the serious historian, his account of such strange rites as those celebrated in honour of the goddess of Mildew in April (4.905ff) are invaluable. And while we may question the strict accuracy of some of Ovid's descriptions – such as that of the rites of the February Lupercalia (2.267ff), a prototype of the modern Valentine's Day – such colourful accounts give life to the dry notices and records of Roman religion in the age of Augustus.

Artistically arranged among these traditional features of the Roman calendar, however, are the erotically charged stories that we have come to expect from Ovid and his elegiac poetry. Venus herself is designated as the 'Miss April' of Ovid's *Calendar*, but stories of sex, seduction – and even rape – feature prominently in each of the six months covered in his poem. So, in January Ovid tells the story of the lecherous Priapus and his frustrated attempts to sleep with the nymph Lotis (1.391-440); in February he tells of the god Mercury's rape of the nymph Lara (2.583-616); in March we hear of the rape of Rhea Silvia (3.11-48) and the Sabine women (3.187-234); in April the mythical rape of Persephone by Pluto (4.417-54); in May the rape of Europa by Jupiter (5.603-20); and in June Priapus again and his unsuccessful attempt to rape the goddess Vesta.

Feminist critic Amy Richlin has pointed to the similarities in style and tone between the rape stories in the *Calendar* and similar accounts of rape in the *Art of Love*. Noting the provocative tone of Ovid's 'political' or 'historical' rape narratives and the comic spirit in which he presents his 'mythical' rapes, she observes that in both the *Calendar* and in the *Art of Love* Ovid represents rape and sexual violence as something that women desire and even 'ask for'. The *praeceptor amoris* insisted that 'force (*uis*) is pleasing to girls' (1.673) and that a girl who goes home untouched 'when she could have been forced' (1.677) will be sad – even though she may pretend to be pleased. In the *Calendar*, too, Ovid highlights the positive outcomes and 'happy endings' that attend his 'mythological' stories of seduction and rape: Europa gets a continent named after her, Rhea Silvia becomes pregnant with the twins Romulus and Remus, and Lara too gives birth to twins. Similarly, the 'historical' stories of violence against women are represented as positive turning points in the history of Rome: the raped Sabine women bear children to Romulus' sex-starved men and thereby establish the future stock of the Roman race, and Lucretia serves as the catalyst that drives Brutus to overthrow the Roman monarchy and establish the Roman republic.

In the *Art of Love*, Ovid frequently insisted that his provocative poem was 'just a joke' (*iocus*). In the *Calendar* too, he repeatedly represents his stories of frustrated desire and fumbled attempts at 'seduction' as comic tales (*ioci*). The lecherous Priapus – popularly depicted in Roman art with a huge and constantly erect phallus – provides Ovid with the comic hero for two almost identical stories in the *Calendar*, and in both the frustrated would-be lover/rapist is exposed to laughter and ridicule. In the *Art of Love*, the *praeceptor* advised his female readers to avoid getting drunk and falling asleep at parties, cautioning that any woman who does so deserves whatever she gets – implicitly warning that in such a state she is likely to be raped. In the *Calendar*, the settings for the two Priapus stories are wild parties involving drinking and dancing, and in both Priapus' erotic targets are women who have fallen asleep.

The links here between the *Calendar* and Ovid's previous erotic writings are clear. But as in his earlier elegiac works, Ovid is eager to proclaim the innovative nature of his poetry in the *Calendar*, declaring in the second book (2.3-10; 15f):

Now, my elegiacs, for the first time you set off in full sail.
     I know that up until now your work has been trivial.
I thought of you as easy ministers of love,
     When I played with your verse in my early years.

Now I sing of sacred rites and the days of the calendar:
   Who would have thought this could come from that?
This is my military service. I carry the only weapons I can.
   But my right hand is not completely useless.

With an eager heart, I still celebrate your name Caesar,
   And follow your path to fame.

Here Ovid adopts the pose of an elegiac poet offering a conventional *recusatio* or justification for his choice of literary form. He claims that his elegiac poetry is his 'military service', the fulfilment of his civic duty to Augustus and to Rome, and that – although unsuited to the soldier's life – his right arm will wield a pen with the same patriotic zeal and devotion that a soldier in the Roman army might wield a weapon. No longer a soldier in Love's army, making love not war as in the *Loves*, Ovid once again likens his elegiac poetry to a kind of warfare, and himself to a Roman soldier dutifully serving Augustus.

At first glance, Ovid's choice of the Roman calendar as the frame and subject for his *Calendar* appears to be politically neutral – or, at least, less politically provocative than his choice of material for the erotic elegies. But Augustan politics and imperial authority had, by the time Ovid came to write the *Calendar*, exerted so complete an influence over Rome that nothing – not even the calendar – had escaped appropriation into the new Augustan ideology. As part of Augustus' extensive public building programme in Rome, the emperor had commissioned an altar to peace, the *Ara Pacis* (whose decorative images celebrated Augustus' links with Rome's past and the peace and prosperity he promised for Rome's future), an immense Mausoleum for himself and the imperial family, and an enormous sundial on the Campus Martius, the *Horologium* (its gnomon formed from a 50 ft Egyptian obelisk,

4. The Calendar

taken from Egypt after Augustus' victory over Antony and Cleopatra), designed to cast its shadow upon both the *Ara Pacis* and the Mausoleum on the date of the yearly autumnal equinox, 23 September – the emperor's birthday.

In addition to this highly visible symbol of the emperor's domination over space and time – over foreign territories such as Egypt and Rome itself, and over the past, present, and future – Rome's calendar of religious festivals and public holidays, anniversaries, and days allotted for political or legal business was also remodelled by Augustus. As *Pontifex Maximus* or Chief High Priest, Augustus held the political and religious authority to determine which days of the calendar would be celebrated as religious holidays and festivals, which days would be designated market days or days when it would be legal to conduct judicial and government business – and on which days it would not. Some anniversaries and major religious festivals were fixed in the yearly calendar but others were moveable feasts, the date of which had to be decided by Rome's senior priests – with Augustus' approval. Every ninth day was officially a market day, but these days moved every year, making it necessary for Augustus and his priests to determine the other days on which it would be legal or illegal, *fas* or *nefas*, to conduct judicial and government business.

Effectively, then, through his senior priests Augustus was able to assert his authority upon every aspect of the Roman calendar. Moreover, by the time of his death, he had added almost fifty new public holidays to the 355-day Julian calendar, marking days to celebrate the anniversaries of his own military victories and significant political acts, those of his father Julius Caesar, and selected *festa domestica* or family festivals. It would have been impossible for Ovid to write about the Roman calendar without referring to these new holidays and recording their Augustan associations. It would have been difficult too for Ovid not to have been aware that he risked causing serious offence to the emperor in his elegiac treatment of these politically sensitive celebrations. Indeed, it is important to notice that, while Ovid's poem takes its title from the *dies fasti* (from which the Roman calendar itself draws its name) in an ostensibly straightforward way, a characteristically Ovidian play upon the root of the word *fasti* – meaning 'legal' and 'allowed', but also 'speech' – allows the title of his poem to be read as a provocative and playful allusion to 'free speech'. Ovid writes, then, an elegiac poem on the subject of the Roman calendar but also on the theme of free speech in Augustan Rome – a highly controversial topic, and an ironic one given his subsequent fate.

However, the risk of offending the emperor in the *Calendar* was moderated somewhat by the deterministic nature of the calendar itself. Although Ovid was free to put his own elegiac spin on his subject material, the material itself was largely dictated to him by the shape and content of the calendar. Indeed, Ovid's silence after 30 June can be interpreted as one of his most daringly provocative political gestures. For in ending his poem at this point he blankly and boldly refuses to speak or write about the otherwise unavoidable months – and patrons – of July and August.

Yet, readers of the *Calendar* have observed that Ovid takes the opportunity to offer praise and ideological backing to Augustus on many more occasions than might seem to be strictly necessary. Geraldine Herbert-Brown, for example, has noted that in Book 2 of the *Calendar* Ovid lavishly honours Augustus' ambitious building and restoration programme, eulogising the emperor as *templorum positor* and *templorum repostor* – builder and restorer of temples (2.55-64):

At the start of the month, Sospita, neighbour of the Phrygian
                                                                            mother
Is said to have been endowed with new shrines.

Where are they now, the temples that were dedicated to the
                                                        goddess
    On that day? They have collapsed over time.
So that other temples might not fall and similarly sink into ruin
    The sacred leader has taken care.
Under him shrines do not feel old age.
    It is not enough that men are indebted to him, so too are
                                                        the gods.
Builder of temples, sacred restorer of temples,
    I pray that the gods may take care of you as well.

Ovid's flattering celebration of Augustus' scheme of renovation, through which many of Rome's dilapidated shrines and temples had been restored, is made on the date of 1 February – yet nothing about these achievements or these titles, or indeed any other Augustan title, achievement, or anniversary, links Augustus to this date. There is, then, no formal requirement or obligation upon Ovid for this tribute to Augustus to appear at the start of the second book of the *Calendar* as it does. But this fact does not necessarily signify the poet's unambiguous support for Augustus and his regime. Some readers may observe an element of equivocation and even implicit sarcasm in the idea that the 'generosity' of Augustus has made not only all men indebted to him, but also all the gods. In fact, scholars have recently suggested that far from offering an unambiguous and uncomplicated tribute to Augustus and his regime, Ovid's *Calendar* is composed in such a way that it can be seen to present a flattering Augustan encomium *and* an implicit criticism of Augustan authority and ideology. Ovid's reputation as an author of playful and politically provocative, if not actively subversive, poetry certainly encourages readers of the *Calendar* to look beneath the surface of its Augustan veneer and to examine the potential inconsistencies and contradictions of the text – and of Ovid's treatment of Augustus.

Ovid's representation of the emperor Augustus as the direct descendant of Venus is one area of potential provocation and play in the *Calendar*. In the development of his public image, Augustus played heavily upon his associations with Venus, emphasising the family connection through Venus' identification as *Genetrix* or founder-mother of the Julian line. In the Forum Augustum, completed in 2 BC, and the temple of Mars the Avenger, statues and images of Venus were featured prominently, and in Virgil's epic *Aeneid*, Venus is represented as the protective mother of Aeneas and thus the mother of the Roman people. Official Augustan representations of the goddess accented this maternal role above others, highlighting Venus' status as nurturing mother and protective parent in the divine form of *Venus Genetrix* – and downplaying her more traditional role as the goddess of Love.

But in his love poetry Ovid had already played heavily upon his own relationship with Venus, emphasising the goddess' associations with love and sex, and her assumed role as patron of love poets. In both the *Loves* and *Art of Love*, Venus had featured prominently, addressed in the *Loves* as '*tenerorum mater Amorum*' or 'Mother of tender Love' (3.15.1). In the prologue to the *Art of Love*, Ovid had formally appealed to the goddess as the source of his divine authority on the theme of *amor*, claiming: 'Venus has chosen me to be the artist of tender love' (1.7). Most provocatively, he had even prayed to her for inspiration for his poem on the arts of love, addressing her again as the '*mater Amoris*' or 'mother of Love' (1.30), playfully combining her two familiar Augustan roles as divine mother and heavenly lover. In the *Calendar*, the combination of these two roles was to prove a far more politically sensitive issue. Having previously focused upon Venus' identity as a playful goddess of love and sex in the *Loves* and *Art of Love*, Ovid was now required to reconcile his own frivolous image of an erotic goddess with Augustus' respectable image of maternal sobriety.

As we might expect, Ovid sails very close to the wind in his description of the religious rituals and ceremonies associated with Venus which traditionally took place in Rome during the month of April. According to Ovid's entry for the first (or the *Kalends*) of April, on this day 'upper-class' Roman women traditionally took part in a ritual which involved the ceremonious undressing of the cult statue of Venus, before washing and decorating it with flowers and myrtle wreaths. Women from the lower classes would take part in a parallel ritual which involved undressing and bathing themselves in the men's public baths. The aetiology that Ovid offers for this first ritual involves a story in which Venus herself, having just bathed in the sea, was once forced to protect her modesty and cover her nakedness from the eyes of lustful satyrs with a screen of myrtle leaves. Although Ovid remarks upon Venus' modesty and chastity in this account, he emphatically and playfully focuses upon her nudity, and although he excludes the goddess from the bathing ritual for common women, he provocatively includes courtesans and prostitutes or *meretrices* among the respectable noble women or *matronae* who traditionally attended Venus' statue on this holy day.

What is more, in a poem designed and conceived – ostensibly at least – as a tribute to Augustus, his family, and his achievements, any reference in the *Calendar* to Venus might be seen as an allusion to Augustus' divine ancestor, and any hint of impropriety or lasciviousness associated with the goddess might be viewed as an insult to her illustrious descendant. Yet, always provocative, Ovid draws attention to this intimate connection between Augustus and Venus, explicitly inviting Caesar to see the fourth month and the fourth book of the *Calendar*, dedicated to Venus, as the most personally significant part of the calendar and the poem – forgetting, it would seem, Augustus' potential self-interest in his own month (4.19f):

> If any part of the calendar ought to interest you
>   Caesar, you have in April what you are concerned with.

Ovid is not oblivious to the challenge he faces in dedicating April to Venus, then, and recognises the risk of insulting the emperor that he and his poem run. Nevertheless, his representation of Venus in the *Calendar* contains a number of important incongruities and inconsistencies that may be interpreted as signs of irreverence and even rebellion against the Augustan regime.

In the opening proem to the fourth book, marking the month of April, Ovid offers an invocation to Venus, dedicating the month of April to her (4.1-6):

> 'O nurturing mother of the twin Loves,' I said, 'favour me.'
>   She turned her face towards her poet:
> 'What do you want with me?' she said. 'Surely you were going to
>   sing of
>   Nobler subjects. Or do you have an old wound in your
>   tender heart?'
> 'Goddess,' I replied, 'you know all about wounds.' She laughed,
>   and
>   Straight away the sky was serene in that part.

Significantly, Venus is addressed in the opening line, not as the 'nurturing mother' of Augustus or the Roman people as we might expect, but as the 'mother of Love'. Immediately, then, Ovid signals that he has in mind the same erotic Venus, goddess of love and sex, whom he had previously addressed in this style in his elegiac love poetry. Indeed, the fact that Ovid's erotic poetry and his elegiac *Calendar* share the same metre further invites the readers of this poem to see the Venus of the *Calendar* as Ovid's elegiac goddess – playful, powerful, and sexy. And her continuing influence over Ovid's poetic career further helps to explain why a poem based on the Roman calendar should include so many erotic elements. According to a literary tradition established by the Greek poet Callimachus, Ovid then engages Venus in conversation, reminding the goddess – and his readers – of their past relationship and of Venus' support for both his loves and his love poetry. This laughing Venus is emphatically Ovid's own elegiac Venus, a point that is underscored in the prologue when Ovid begins to explain why April and the fourth book of his *Calendar* are being dedicated to her, and why she is his 'Miss April' (4.13f):

> We have come to the fourth month, in which you are most
> > celebrated:
> > You know Venus that both the poet and the month belong
> > > to you.

Yet, traditionally, the fourth month did *not* belong to Venus. According to the Roman calendars used by Ovid to form the foundation of his *Calendar*, April was neither named after nor especially associated with Venus. So, Ovid is required to offer a detailed aetiological and etymological explanation for this odd and innovative assertion. In a style that he has practised in the previous three books of the *Calendar*, Ovid suggests that April did indeed take its name from Venus – although not from the Latin, but rather from the Greek form of her name: Aphrodite, a word which is itself etymologically derived from the Greek word for 'sea spray' (4.61f):

> But I deduce that the month of Venus was named in the Greek
> > language:
> > The goddess is named after the spray of the sea.

He makes a further tenuous connection between Venus and the month of April, incorporating the more traditional Roman etymological derivation of *Aprilis* from the Latin *aperire* (to spring open) in his claim that (4.125-8):

> No time was more fitting to Venus than spring:
>> In spring the earth gleams, in spring the soil is loose;
> Now the plants lift pointed shoots pushed up through the soil,
>> Now the blossom drives the bud through the swelling bark.

In a related celebration of the goddess' associations with reproduction, he also offers an elaborate – and overstated – description of Venus as sovereign of the world (4.91-5):

> Indeed, she deservedly rules the whole world;
>> She owns a kingdom greater than any god,
> She gives laws to heaven and earth and her birthplace, the sea,
>> And through her every species keeps going.
> She created all the gods (too many to list).

This exaggerated account of Venus' power might seem to offer an enthusiastic tribute to the goddess and to her descendent Augustus (who might more legitimately be said to rule the whole world, own a kingdom greater than any god, and give laws to all). But the implicit source of Venus' universal power and authority in this eulogy is sex. Gods, men, and animals of every kind are created and governed by Venus because, in Ovid's account, she is the divine embodiment of Sex. So, far from redeeming Venus as a respectable Augustan matron in his prologue to Book 4, Ovid gently reminds his audience that the mother of Aeneas, Romulus, Augustus, and the entire Roman race is not only the goddess of tender Love but also the goddess of Sex. Critics have observed, moreover, that Ovid seems to protest rather *too* much about the goddess' right to give her name and patronage to the fourth month, insisting upon the authenticity and authority of his representation of Venus, despite its obvious inconsistencies and incongruities. Is it possible, perhaps, that in drawing attention to the inconsistencies of his own image of Venus, Ovid is subtly drawing attention to the incongruities of Augustus' image of the goddess, obliquely commenting upon the tension and irony implied in a champion of family values honouring a goddess of love and sex, and a divine adulteress? If so, Ovid's provocation of Augustus was not to remain unchecked for much longer.

5

Sad Songs

Let us imagine a ruin – say, of some small Greek temple
    in an out of the way place, where the god happened
to speak or spare or warn or simply to show herself,
    nearly leveled, say by an earthquake, but one
single column left, still holding up its corner
    by which we can imagine the rest of the structure.
Which is the more affecting, the ruined part of the building,
    or that surviving piece of it, forlorn,
bereaved of the rest? My life is the ruin; yours, dear wife,
    is that still-standing beautiful pillar, vessel
for the spirit that yet abides. How else to declare
    my love for you, who deserve a less wretched
though not a better or more adoring husband? My powers
    are not what they were. Clumsy sincerity
must speak with its thick tongue, stammering out thanks
    and affection, unadorned but still heartfelt.

                                    David Slavitt, *Tristia* 1. 6

In AD 8, on holiday on the island of Elba, Ovid received the sudden
news that Augustus had ordered his banishment or *relegatio*, that he
was not to be allowed to live in Rome, and that his books were to
be publicly banned. Ovid was to be permitted to keep his property
and possessions, but not to choose the location of his effective exile;
he was to spend an unspecified period – which turned out to be the
rest of his life – in a place as geographically, socially, and culturally
far from Rome as Ovid could have feared. He was banished to

Tomis, a cold and austere outpost on the western shore of the Black Sea, on the edge of the Roman Empire and the edge of the civilised world. For an urbane, cultured, and emphatically *Roman* poet, whose work had been inspired by the people and politics of Rome, Rome's *mores* and morals, Roman lifestyles and Roman literature, to be banished from Rome itself was a harsh sentence, but to be sent to Tomis, an inhospitable settlement of armed barbarians who spoke no Latin and only a rare Greek dialect, was a particularly cruel – and apt – form of punishment.

One response to his effective exile – and one possible motive for Augustus' choice of punishment – might have been for Ovid to stop writing poetry. With no immediate audience, encouragement, or familiar sources of inspiration, it would not have been surprising if Ovid's removal from Rome had marked the end of his active literary career. Yet, in literary terms, Ovid appears to have thrived in his new environment. Initially, in the *Tristia*, or *Sad Songs*, he writes of his inability to communicate with the local Tomitians, to whom he – ironically Rome's greatest living poet – seems the unintelligible barbarian (5.10.37). Subsequently, however, he tells us that he gave public readings of his works, and even learned the native Greek dialect or Getic language spoken by the local people, attempting, he claims, to write some poetry in it. Indeed, he describes one incongruous (and possibly imagined) scene in which he gives a public recitation of a poem composed in Latin metre – elegy perhaps – but in the local Getic language, to an assembly of barbarian locals who brandish their weapons in appreciation of his work (*Letters from Pontus* 4.13).

In Latin and in his favourite elegiac metre, Ovid was to compose nine books of poetic letters or verse epistles during his period of banishment, five collected in the *Sad Songs* and a further four in the *Letters from Pontus*. He addresses several poems to his friends, asking them to appeal to the emperor on his behalf and to help secure his return to Rome. But the person to and about whom he writes most often is his wife, who had remained in Rome – perhaps because Ovid's banishment was assumed only to be temporary, or perhaps to spare her the uncomfortable and unhealthy living conditions offered by Tomis. In these poems he complains repeatedly of the snow and extreme cold, and of the illnesses and minor pains that torment him, but he also reflects upon his loneliness and, in particular, his suffering in the absence of his wife – she who, he writes, is dearer to him than everything in the world. In this new setting, Ovid exploits the elegiac tropes of love as a disease and as something that brings pain, to represent himself as a loving husband – suffering now as he once 'suffered' in his *Loves*. And, in particular, he plays up the 'cold' frigidity of Tomis as a figure for his isolation and unhappiness – still a potent metaphor in modern love songs, from the White Stripes' 'In the cold, cold, night', to Nico's 'Roses in the snow'.

In *Sad Songs* 4.3, Ovid describes a moonless starlit night and pictures the same stars shining over both Tomis and Rome, wondering if his wife sees them too – and if she is thinking of him. The poet David Slavitt's translation reflects the tone of the original beautifully (*Tristia* 4.3.13-34):

> Is my wife there? Is she looking out, thinking of me?
>   What, if the stars could speak, would they report?
> Would I really want to know? Or dare? I swear I would.
>   One must have faith in unwavering faith. Polaris
> would be less likely to wander than she. I don't need
>   the testimony of stars to what I already
> know in the depths of my heart to be certain and true. She
>   thinks of me and says her name aloud,
> which is my name too, and gazes at my portrait
>   to speak to me of her love. Providing only

that she is alive tonight, her love is alive.
  And if those stars could speak to her, they'd say,
when her heart is heavy, having braved its griefs all day,
    and woe sneaks up at night when she lays her head
on the pillow we used to share, that I love her still
    and wish I could reach out my hand to comfort
her tossing body. Our love expresses itself in aches
    instead of pleasures; morning's weary bones
are a parody of past mornings when, after passion,
    we'd drag ourselves from bed. The torture is all
we have left these days. It's what Andromache felt,
    watching Hector's body hauled in the dust.

Readers familiar with Ovid's *Loves* and *Heroines' Letters* might hear
in this poem echoes of Ovid's earlier elegiac writing. Indeed, this
elegiac epistle would not seem out of place set among either of
these collections. In the Latin poem, Ovid addresses his wife as his
domina or mistress (4.3.9), just as he referred to Corinna in the
Loves. He pictures his wife sleeping alone in the bed that they used
to share with the same pathos with which Ariadne describes herself
in the *Heroines' Letters*, waking on a moonlit night in an empty bed
to find Theseus gone. Ovid even employs a mythological allusion
here: a device that so often seemed intrusive and artificial in the
love songs but that here seems both apt and sincere. Ovid's sad
songs, then, seem very like his love songs.

  Yet, in the opening poem of the first book of the *Sad Songs*,
Ovid declares explicitly that the attitude and style of his new
elegiac poetry will be very different from the old – that he has
himself undergone a metamorphosis like one of the characters
from his epic (1.1.119-22):

    … among those transformed bodies
      The shape of my own fate can be related.

5. Sad Songs

For that has suddenly become altered from what it was before,
Now a cause for weeping, at another time a cause for joy.

This statement draws a clear distinction between the new exilic elegy, with its themes of sorrow and lament, and the erotic elegy of his earlier work, with its themes of love and sex. In fact, Ovid appears eager to discriminate particularly between this new elegiac project and the disgraced *Art of Love*, represented here as cowering in the shadows upon the shelves containing the poet's other books (1.1.109-12). Critics and readers – even those suspicious of every truth claim Ovid makes in the quasi-autobiographical *Loves* and *Art of Love* – tend to accept this new position without challenge. Paul Veyne, one of Ovid's most sceptical readers, considers that Ovid tells us nothing about his 'real' life or 'real' loves in the *Loves*, but he accepts without question the autobiographical details that Ovid offers us in the exile poems. So, when Ovid claims in the *Sad Songs* and *Letters from Pontus* that he has turned his back upon the frivolous love poetry of his youth, Veyne believes him:

The unhappy poet no longer thinks about being amusing or entertaining. His elegies are now nothing more than lamentations, supplications, curses, and petitions for mercy.

But Veyne is wrong. Ovid's situation has radically changed but the self-styled 'poet of tender Love' has not. Readers of Ovid's other books – specifically, his *Metamorphoses* – may remember that the victims of transformation in this poem were altered in external appearance alone, and retained their essential human identity and character despite their physical metamorphosis. The shape and look of Ovid's own poetry and fate may have been metamorphosed as a result of Augustus' punishment, but he hints here that the poet

97

has survived this transformation, and that his essential poetic identity and familiar Ovidian character may still be traced in this new
guise. So, although the poet maintains that 'I am not who I once
was' (3.11.25), it is clear that the exiled *ego* who speaks these words
in the *Sad Songs* is recognisable as the same elegiac *ego* of Ovid's
earlier love poetry.

Ovid's own metamorphosis and that of his elegy in the exile
poems are most clearly demonstrated in one of the *Letters from
Pontus*, a metapoetic revision of the opening poem of *Loves* Book
1 in which, nearing the end of his literary career, the poet looks
back to its beginning. In this poem, Love or Cupid – the playful
source of inspiration for Ovid's love poetry – once again pays a visit
to his poet, but just as exile has altered the poet, so too has Cupid
changed (3.3.5-20):

It was night, and the moon was entering the double-shuttered
windows
As she is accustomed to shine in the middle of the month.
Sleep, the common rest from sorrow, held me,
And my languid limbs were stretched across the whole bed,
When suddenly the air shimmered with beating of wings,
And a slight creak sounded as the window was opened.
Terrified, I raised myself up, leaning on my left arm,
And sleep was driven from my trembling breast.
There stood Love, but not with the look he used to have,
Sadly touching his left hand upon the maple bedpost,
No necklace at his throat, no brooch clipped in his hair,
Nor were his locks carefully arranged as before.
The soft hair hung down over his shabby face,
His feathers seemed to my eyes scruffy,
Like those on the back of the flying dove,
Which too many hands have patted and touched.

5. Sad Songs

In this poem, Ovid draws an unambiguous parallel between himself and Love; both have suffered since their first meeting in the poet's youth, both have lost their 'innocence' and their playfulness, and both now are *tristis* or sad. The image of degradation and decline that Ovid recognises in Love's squalid physical appearance, moreover, reflects the avowed deterioration of his elegiac poetry. The difference between his past light-hearted erotic elegy and his present sorrowful exilic elegy is dramatically highlighted by the eroticised setting of Cupid's visit. In a scene highly reminiscent of *Loves* 1.5 in which Corinna appears in Ovid's shuttered bedroom for an afternoon of sex, Ovid lies languidly on his bed, the moonlight filtered through the shutters, when a bedraggled Cupid unexpectedly appears. But the similarities between these two scenes throw their dissimilarities into high relief: midday has become night; a pale Tomitian moon rather than Roman sunlight enters through the shutters; in the place of Corinna's naked beauty, a bedraggled Cupid; in place of playful lovemaking and *amor*, sad and squalid *Amor*. The transformation of the author of the *Loves*, his divine patron, and his love elegy is a sad sight indeed.

In the proem to the fifth and final book of the *Sad Songs*, Ovid offers his most explicit declaration that he has rejected the tropes of erotic elegy in his exile poetry, claiming that he has now turned his back upon the happy themes of his youth and that he will now write sad songs as befits his new condition (5.1.5f; 15-20):

> Sorrowful is my position, so sorrowful is my song,
> The work is suited to its material.

> If anyone seeks the delights of lascivious poetry,
> I forewarn you, do not read this.
> Gallus will be better, or Propertius with his sweet lips,
> Better the friendly genius Tibullus.

And I wish that I were not counted among them.
Alas, why was my Muse ever playful?

The appearance of this pronouncement at such a late point in the
collection and the poet's claim to 'forewarn' his readers, however,
suggests that we should not interpret Ovid's declaration as
applying to the previous four books or to the *Sad Songs* as a whole.
Ovid can hardly have expected his readers to respond seriously to
his avowed wish *not* to be counted among the canon of great Latin
love elegists, when he had unequivocally included himself among
their number in the preceding poem (4.10.53f):

Tibullus was your successor, Gallus, and Propertius was his;
I myself came after these, the fourth in the series.

In his poems from exile, then, Ovid does not simply reject the
themes and tropes of Roman love poetry. He reconfigures the
traditional elegiac codes and conventions of erotic love and desire
– at the same time both experimenting with the elegiac genre,
pushing its boundaries into untried territory, and returning to
elegy's ancient origins as a medium for songs of sorrow and lament.
Freed from the more conventional elegiac contexts of romantic
and sexual love, Ovid's exilic poetry shows how elegy can offer a
powerful poetic vehicle through which to examine universal
themes of love and loss. Yet, as critics Stephen Harrison and
Gareth Williams have demonstrated, whereas the elegiac writing of
Ovid's career pre-exile was characterised by the poet's claims of
literary innovation and elevation, the *Sad Songs* and *Letters from
Pontus* have often been characterised as the inferior works of a
poetic genius in decline.

In the twentieth century, this self-assessment of Ovid's later
works was too often accepted uncritically, although recent schol-

arship has helped to demonstrate that the poet's pose of creative deterioration in the exile poems is precisely a poetic pretence – akin to the conventional *recusatio* offered in the pre-exile elegiac poetry as an excuse not to write epic on the grounds of poetic incapacity. In fact, Ovid's exile poetry, while markedly different from the erotic elegy in tone and content, is far from its inferior and can be seen to mark the poet's welcome return to elegy after his adventures with epic in the *Metamorphoses* – a kind of literary homecoming for the exiled poet. In the *Sad Songs* and *Letters from Pontus*, Ovid also turns again to the verse epistle, building upon the innovative and experimental work begun in the *Heroines' Letters*. But this is not the only – or even the principal – Ovidian text to be revisited and reviewed in the poems from exile. In these poems, Ovid repeatedly recasts familiar erotic tropes, ingeniously reworking and re-energising the elegiac themes of his former career.

So, in *Letters from Pontus* 2.2 Ovid evokes the language of the elegiac locked out lover to represent the exiled poet as an *exclusus amator*, barred not from his mistress' bedroom but from Augustus' Rome. In a letter to Messalinus, the poet begs his friend to plead his case to Augustus' hard-hearted successor, Tiberius – just as an elegiac lover might beg a doorkeeper or slave to plead his case to a hard-hearted mistress (2.2.39f). Here, as elsewhere in the exile poems, Ovid imports some of the erotic precepts of the dishonoured *Art of Love*. He transforms erotodidactic instructions upon how to seduce a lover into advice upon how to 'seduce' the emperor and his wife – and so secure Ovid's recall to Rome (*Letters from Pontus* 1.2.67-128; 3.1.129-66).

In *Sad Songs* 3.3 Ovid reworks a traditional elegiac premise in which the poet writes to his absent mistress – here the poet's wife – describing his failing health and predicting his imminent demise. Here, as elsewhere in the exile poems, Ovid transforms conventional elegiac metaphors of love as a sickness, to give colour to his physical sufferings in exile. The poem has been seen as a variant upon a theme most famously explored by Ovid's predecessor Tibullus, whose elegy 1.3 similarly contains a poetic epitaph, which the poet morbidly imagines may mark his grave. But parallels may also be seen between Ovid's morbid elegy in the *Sad Songs* and some of the elegies in his own *Heroines' Letters*. Several of the abandoned heroines imagine that their death is imminent and reflect morosely upon their sad fate, while Phyllis and Dido – like Ovid – end their epistles by writing their own poetic epitaphs. The *Sad Songs* poem shares several distinctive features with the verse poems of the *Heroines' Letters*, including its opening lines, in which the poet self-consciously 'explains' to his wife that he is too ill to write – although not too sick to 'dictate' an eighty-eight line letter in elegiac verse (3.3.1-4):

> If you happen to wonder why this letter of mine
> Is written in another's hand, I am ill.
> Ill in an unknown place at the ends of the earth,
> And I am unsure yet of my recovery.

This deliberate opening echoes the opening lines to the letters of Briseis, Canace, and Sappho in the *Heroines' Letters*, who similarly comment self-consciously upon the handwriting and presentation of their epistles. Like many of his heroines, Ovid goes on to complain about the fact of being ill so far away from his own home and from those who love and care for him. He laments – like Ariadne (10.119-24) – that if he dies now he will not be buried in his native soil or receive proper funeral rites, that no one will weep over him or close his eyes (3.3.37-46). He worries, like his heroines, that as he lies ill – and even dying – his love has already forgotten him and is living happily without him (3.3.25f):

5. Sad Songs

So, while I am uncertain about living, are you perhaps
    Spending time pleasurably, forgetting about me?

Yet, unlike his heroines, Ovid is confident that his wife is as miserable without him as he is without her (3.3.27f):

No you are not, I swear. This is clear to me, my dearest,
    That you spend no time without me that is not sad.

In fact, it is evident in this poem that Ovid has recast a number of the characteristic elegiac tropes associated with this theme: his beloved wife, unlike the lovers of the abandoned women of the *Heroines' Letters*, has not forsaken him; he has not been deceived by her and is not unsure of her love. His epitaph attributes no blame to anyone as the cause of his death and he appears to have taken a traditional elegiac theme and transformed it into a subject fitting for his collection of sad songs.

Ovid's exilic reworking of the erotic themes of love elegy is poignantly demonstrated in the centrepiece of Book 1 of the *Sad Songs*, a love poem dedicated not to an elegiac mistress but to an elegiac poet's wife. Here, the poet compares his wife with the mythical exemplars of female virtue and chastity, Andromache, Laodamia, and, above all, Penelope – the first lady of his *Heroines' Letters* – declaring that she surpasses them all in her goodness. He even goes as far as to claim that she might depose Penelope from her position as the first of Ovid's elegiac heroines (1.6.19-28):

In virtue, neither Hector's wife, nor Laodamia,
    Her husband's companion in death, comes before you.
If fate had granted you Homer as your poet,
    Penelope's story would be second to yours.
Then you would hold first place among the respected 'heroines',
    You would be regarded first in the goodness of your heart,

Whether you owe this to yourself, made virtuous by no teacher,
   But given such morals at the moment of your birth,
Or whether the first of women, respected by you for so many

                                     years,
   Teaches you to be the model of a good wife.

In its transformation of traditional elegiac tropes, most obviously in metamorphosing the figure of the poet's mistress into the far more respectable figure of his own wife, this poem appears to support Ovid's claims to have distanced himself from erotic elegy. A virtuous *matrona* has replaced the licentious *meretrix* of Ovid's love elegy, and unlike the mistress who sought to fleece her lover for everything possible, Ovid's wife protects his financial interests in Rome, defending his property from the 'wolves' and 'vultures' who would seize it. In contrast to the elegiac *puella* who has learned from Ovid's *Art of Love* how to seduce and deceive her lovers, his wife has an innate knowledge of love and loyalty – or has possibly learned from Livia, the emperor's own consort, how to be the model of a perfect wife. In this way, the poet can be seen to pay a subtle tribute to Augustus and Livia in this poem addressed to his wife, emphasising the renunciation of his former provocative ways and the transformation of his erotic elegy in exile. He intimates that his exile poetry may be regarded as superior to his erotic elegy in both quality and virtue, in the same way that his wife is superior to his elegiac heroines in respect of her domestic qualities and virtues.

Yet, closer reading of this poem suggests that while Ovid's approach to elegy may have changed in exile, some aspects of his characteristic style of elegy remain fundamentally the same. Ovid addresses his wife in a style familiar from his poems to Corinna in the *Loves*, promising her – as he promised Corinna, and as all the Roman love poets promised their mistresses – that his poetry will make her immortal (1.6.35f):

5. Sad Songs

And so far as my praise has any power,
You will live for all time in my poetry.

But in this bold assertion, repeated in subsequent exile poems (*Sad Songs* 4.3.81f; 5.14.1-6), Ovid is not simply reversing the tenet of a traditional elegiac trope by replacing a *meretrix* with a *matrona* as the subject of his poetic immortalisation. In promising to bestow immortal praise and fame upon Corinna in the *Loves*, Ovid actively and provocatively rejected the opportunity to bestow such favours upon Augustus, choosing to commemorate not Rome's emperor and empire but a mere girl. In the *Sad Songs*, he similarly elects to eschew the opportunity to celebrate Augustus' virtues and triumphs, this time in order to pay tribute to the virtues and achievements of his wife. Moreover, having examined the possible source of his wife's great virtue, Ovid laments that he and his poetry lack the power to justly pay tribute to her merits (1.6.29f):

Alas, my poems do not have the power,
And my lips are unequal to your merits.

After claiming so many times in his previous elegiac career that his poems did not have the power to sing of *Augustus* and his achievements and that his elegiac verse was unequal to the task of celebrating Rome's emperor, Ovid now returns to one of the central tropes of his erotic elegy and in place of the *princeps* once again sets a *puella*.

A further six elegies in the *Sad Songs* and another two in the *Letters from Pontus* return to the theme of Ovid's love for his absent wife (*Sad Songs* 1.6, 3.3, 4.3, 5.2, 5.5, 5.11, 5.14 and *Letters from Pontus* 1.4, 3.1). These love poems can be interpreted as straightforward reworkings of familiar erotic themes from Roman love poetry, substituting for the character of the erotic *domina* of elegy

105

the more respectable figure of the *matrona* – as befits a collection of poems designed to convince Augustus of their author's morality, virtue, and reform. Yet, these poems might also – or rather – be read as eroticised representations of themes sponsored by Augustus as part of his programme to promote civic and family values, substituting the provocative persona of the poet-lover with the conciliatory figure of the poet-husband. For Ovid's exilic love poems do not simply renounce the erotic values inherent in the illicit affairs between poet and mistress endorsed by his elegiac poetry. Rather they celebrate the erotic values similarly, though perhaps less obviously, inherent in legitimised relationships between husband and wife. In fact, although Ovid frequently refers to his wife in the *Sad Songs* and *Letters from Pontus* using the familiar Latin words of *uxor* and *coniunx*, he also refers to her repeatedly in the exile poems as his *domina* – that is, in conventional elegiac terms, as his mistress. But Ovid has not simply sanitised an erotic motif, he has subtly eroticised the relationship between a husband and wife. So, while contemporary readings of Ovid's love poems from exile habitually contrast their 'respectable' tone and 'virtuous' content with the licentious indecency of the earlier love poems, they neglect the fact that in the *Sad Songs* and *Letters from Pontus* Ovid offers his readers a rare thing – love poetry inspired by and dedicated to a beloved wife.

Ovid's reworking of traditional elegiac situations and erotic themes – and his celebration of the erotic potential of a marital relationship – is given an explicit political dimension in the *Letters from Pontus* 1.4. Here Ovid reverses the famous conclusion of *Loves* 1.13, in which the approach of Dawn or Aurora is regarded as hateful for bringing to an end a night spent with his mistress and, instead of begrudging Aurora's coming, he now looks forward to the arrival of the day that will reunite him with his wife (1.4.49-58):

O may the gods grant that I will be able to see you in this way,
    And bring loving kisses to your transformed curls,
And embracing your slender body in my arms,
    Say, 'Love for me has made you so thin,'
And between your tears and my tears, be able to tell of my
                                 sufferings,
    Enjoy a conversation I never dared hope for,
And to offer the incense owed by considerate hand
    To the Caesars and the wife worthy of Caesar, true gods.
I pray that Memnon's mother, when the prince is appeased,
    May as soon as possible announce the day with her rosy lips.

Yet, this incongruous vision of Ovid eagerly anticipating the dawn so that he can worship the imperial family is only part of the picture depicted in this poem. The aged and exiled Ovid, in marked contrast to his youthful elegiac counterpart in the *Loves* who prayed for Aurora to slow her pace and grant him more precious time in bed with his beloved mistress, now longs for the dawn to come as quickly as possible. But this is not because Ovid the poet has been utterly transformed by his suffering in exile or because Ovid the lover has been reformed by his banishment. Ovid here prays for the dawn of the day that he is recalled to Rome to come quickly, so that he may be granted precious time with his beloved wife before he dies. He has reversed the tenet of the former trope, but his desire to spend more time in the arms of the woman he loves remains the same.

The programmatic opening elegy of the first book of the *Sad Songs* sets the prevailing political tone for Ovid's exile poems. Here Ovid's detailed directions to his *liber* or book upon how to act when it arrives in Rome reveal some of the tensions and insecurities that torment the exiled poet and characterise his exile poetry. He warns his personified book of elegies to be careful in what it says to the people it meets in Rome – 'take care that you do not happen to say that which there is no need to speak of' (1.1.22); to make no attempt to defend its author against criticism or slander – 'take care that you offer no defence, even if mauled with words' (1.1.25); and, above all, to seek a compassionate audience (1.1.27-30):

> Find someone who sighs over my exile,
>> Who reads your poems with cheeks that do not stay dry,
> And who prays silently to himself, so that no ill-wisher may hear,
>> That with Caesar mollified my punishment may be
>>> lightened.

The caution that Ovid urges upon his little book and his insistence that the book reveal its contents only to a sympathetic reader make plain the poet's apprehension at the reception he and his poetry are likely to receive in Rome. He is, understandably, even more anxious about the reception that the emperor might offer his *liber* and warns his book to be particularly careful in making any approach to Augustus' palace – 'so be careful, my book, and look around with timid heart' (1.1.87). As for attempting to approach the emperor himself, he cautions his book (1.1.92-8):

> ... The situation and the place will give you advice.
> If you can be handed to him when he is at leisure, if you see
>> everything
>> Is peaceful, if his anger has broken its force,
> If there is anyone who will hand you over, speaking just a brief
>> introduction
>> While you are hesitating in fear to go, then go.
> On a good day and with better luck than your own master
>> May you make it there and lighten my misfortunes.

5. Sad Songs

The emphasis upon chance, opportunity, and the emperor's good humour to provide the conditions upon which the book's favourable reception – and Ovid's release – depends is significant. It contributes to the portrayal of Augustus both as a capricious tyrant, unreliable, unforgiving, and unjust, and as a noble prince, approachable, forgiving, and fair. Indeed, throughout the exile poems Ovid's characterisation of the emperor demonstrates such equivocation, and critics of the *Sad Songs* and *Letters from Pontus* have traditionally been divided over whether they viewed Ovid's exilic elegy as pro- or anti-Augustan. More recent scholarship, however, has demonstrated that such rigidly defined terms are inapplicable to Ovid's ambivalent poetic and political stance, and has suggested that readers can find politically subversive elements in those passages of the *Sad Songs* and *Letters from Pontus* that seem most flattering to Augustus *and* that they can detect loyalty to the Augustan regime in those that seem most seditious.

The first two books of the *Sad Songs*, containing the first poems composed in Tomis, are clearly focused upon achieving the poet's aim of returning to Rome as soon as possible – 'booking the return trip' as Stephen Hinds has described it. These poems share a common conviction that it *must* be possible to placate Augustus and persuade him to authorise Ovid's recall to Rome, and with this objective they forcefully represent the poet's misery in exile, his remorse at having offended the emperor, and his brilliance as a poet. But this is not to say that these first two books lack entirely the ironic tone or playful style that characterised Ovid's earlier elegiac writing, or that an attitude of penitence and humility dominates the poems from this initial period of exile.

Book 2 of the *Sad Songs* is particularly significant in this respect. Presented as a single extended poem addressed indirectly to Augustus, this book ostensibly offers Ovid's defence of his *Art of Love* and a plea that the sentence of relegation imposed upon him should be revoked on the grounds that it was unmerited, unjust, and unreasonably severe. The poem – and the poet – is careful to avoid causing the *princeps* further offence by censuring him openly for his injustice and inclemency, however, and focuses its defence rather upon Augustus' misinterpretation of the *Art of Love*. Ingeniously, Ovid first suggests that the emperor cannot have read the *Art of Love* himself (2.215-20):

> Just as Jupiter watching over the gods and the lofty heavens at the
> > same time
> > Has no time to give to the small things,
> So while you look around the world which depends upon you,
> > Little things escape your attention.
> Should you, prince of the world, leave your post
> > To read songs composed in unequal metre?

He lists the many onerous responsibilities that Augustus must bear as leader of the known world; the territories he must defend and the peace-treaties he must broker, the wars against enemies he must fight abroad, and the war against immorality and vice he must fight at home in Rome itself. 'Is it any wonder then, that under this weight of great affairs, you have never unrolled my jokes?' (2.237f), he observes. This representation of Ovid's own work as playful, light-hearted, and humorous (*iocus*) supports an important rhetorical ploy that will form one of the central pillars of the poet's defence of the *Art of Love* – it was never intended to be taken seriously, and Augustus has missed the joke. He has, moreover, either misread the *Art of Love* or not read it at all. The conciliatory yet potentially provocative observation that even Jupiter has too much on his divine agenda to pay attention to little things, reminds Ovid's reader, if not the emperor himself, that the divine Augustus cannot be expected to be a close reader of Ovid's 'little' books.

This damning and provocative indictment of the emperor (or is it another 'joke'?) has been read as an indication that Ovid did not expect or intend Augustus to read this poem. In fact, this might help to explain the audacity of Ovid's professed 'defence' of the *Art of Love* in this poem. He declares that the entire history of poetry – from the Greek poets, Sappho, Callimachus, and Homer to the Roman poets, Catullus, Gallus, Tibullus, and Propertius – has universally been concerned with the subject of love and sex (2.361-470), but that he alone, the 'successor' (2.467) of these great poets, has been punished. With bold irreverence, he argues (2.361f; 2.371-6):

> Furthermore, I am not the only poet to have written about tender
> loves:
>   Though I am the only one to be punished for writing of love.
>
> The *Iliad* itself – what is it but a poem about an adulteress,
>   Over whom her lover and her husband fought?
> What is there in it before passion for Briseis, and
>   The seizing of the girl which causes the anger of the leaders.
> What is the *Odyssey* but a poem about one woman who, for the
>   sake of sex,
>   Is pursued by many suitors while her husband is away?

Employing an ingenious *reductio ad absurdum* (a familiar rhetorical ploy from his erotic elegies), Ovid manipulates the response of his projected reader (here imagined to be the emperor himself) to his own advantage. If Augustus accepts Ovid's characterisation of the canonical works of Greek and Roman literature as poems about tender love (*teneros amores*), then he cannot censure Ovid's *Art of Love* or punish its author for writing upon the same theme. Yet, if Augustus argues that epic poems such as Homer's *Iliad* and

111

Odyssey self-evidently do *not* focus upon tales of adultery and only a particularly biased, perverse, or wrong-headed reader would describe these canonical works as offensive or licentious, then he lays himself open to the charge of being precisely such a biased, perverse, and wrong-headed reader of Ovid's *Art of Love*. And so Ovid's *Sad Songs* proves to be no less provocative in its playful subversion of Augustus and Augustan ideology than the *Art of Love* itself. But whether or not Augustus ever read any of these letters from exile, we will never know. Ovid, the 'poet of tender Love', died in Tomis in AD 17.

Ovid in the Third Millennium

My own view ... is that I was sent packing for being unfaithful to poetry, for not writing the wholesome stuff the Emperor wanted; as the Boss, he owned all that was thought, said or done. To put it in Soviet terms, I had refused to come up with tractor poems, paeans to hydroelectric stations, to the founders of the party, to the rustic rabble and the proles of Rome.

Paul West, 'Nightfall on the Romanian Coast'

Ovid ends the last poem in his first book of elegies with the declaration that even after death, when the funeral pyre has destroyed his body, he will live on (*Loves* 1.15.41f):

So, even when the final flame has destroyed me,
I will live, and a great part of me will survive.

Given that this was written at the start of his literary career, when Ovid was only in his twenties, and echoes the words of the older poet Horace writing at the height of his own fame, this seems a particularly bold claim. Yet, nearly two thousand years after his death, Ovid's confidence in the power of his poetic *corpus* to survive the death and destruction of his physical *corpus* appears to have been justified.

One reason for the continuing readability of Ovid's elegiac writing today may be traced back to the influence of Roman love elegy as a whole, and of Ovid's love songs in particular, upon the history of western love poetry. The Roman love poets, especially Ovid, shaped the medieval tradition of courtly love and the songs that celebrated it. They moulded the love sonnets of Renaissance Europe, including those of Petrarch and Shakespeare, who appropriated the themes and motifs of Latin love poetry for their own writings, just as the Roman elegists had earlier borrowed from the Greeks. They inspired the poetry of eighteenth-century 'Augustan' England, whose poets both translated Roman erotic elegy and styled their own writings upon it, and in turn they influenced the traditions and conventions of love poetry and love songs as we recognise them today.

Through the lyrics of contemporary love songs, a direct line of ancestry can be drawn back to Ovid's erotic elegies. Although the troubadours of the middle ages and the sonneteers of Renaissance Europe were often forced to accommodate the codes and conventions of Ovid's love poems to fit their own frustrated and unconsummated *amores*, Ovid's 'poetry of consummation' – in which love and sex are synonymous – bears an immediate relevance for contemporary writers of postmodern, post-Romantic love songs. Ovid's detached cynicism, his self-deprecating humour, and characteristic playfulness, moreover, are still recognisable in the lyrics of contemporary love songs, from pop to hip-hop.

Although we are far from living in a new 'Age of Ovid' or *aetas Ovidiana* – as the medievalist Ludwig Traube described the flourishing of Latin literature in the twelfth and thirteenth centuries – few classical authors have made such an enduring impact upon the literary, artistic, and imaginative landscapes of Western Europe as Ovid. During the medieval *aetas Ovidiana*, his poetry was far and away the most popular of any classical – or contemporary – writer. Ovid's love songs were used in the medieval schoolroom to teach literary and rhetorical style, the *Calendar* was used to teach history, the *Heroines' Letters* were widely copied as templates for poetic letters, the *Cures for Love* was consulted for medical advice, and – however strange this may now seem – the *Calendar*, *Heroines' Letters*, *Arts of Love* and *Cures for Love* were regarded as authoritative works of philosophy, and were consulted by medieval experts for advice on ethics and the good life.

At the end of the twentieth century, Ovid's popularity saw a new renaissance among contemporary artists, poets, and writers. The *Metamorphoses* featured most prominently in creative works of reception and translation – notably, the collaborative poetic project *After Ovid* and Ted Hughes' *Tales from Ovid* – but a number of modern writers were inspired by Ovid's exile, including David Malouf in *An Imaginary Life*, and Christoph Ransmayr in *The Last World*. Malouf's novel focuses upon Ovid as an exile not simply from Rome but from the language of Rome. In trying to teach a wild boy (who is uncivilised even by the standards of Tomis) the local Getic language, Ovid realises that the language of the Latin letters he is sending back to Rome no longer holds real meaning for him. Malouf's Ovid tries to recover a lost innocence symbolised by his attempts to relearn a lost childhood language. Ransmayr's novel focuses upon the character of Cotta, Ovid's friend and addressee of six of the letters collected in the *Letters from Pontus*, who travels to Tomis in search of the poet. There he finds a land that seems to have been transformed by Ovid's presence and poetry, and whose inhabitants appear to have taken on the identities of characters from the *Metamorphoses* – a land mirroring the literary landscape of postclassical poetry.

In 2000, a number of popular authors, among them Margaret Atwood, A.S. Byatt, and Michèle Roberts, contributed to a collection of innovative and original stories on Ovidian themes in *Ovid Metamorphosed*, experimenting with and reshaping the form of the modern short story – just as Ovid had played with the form of the Roman love elegy two thousand years before. Several of these stories took their inspiration from Ovid's elegiac writing, reworking and recasting Ovid's poetry in new contemporary contexts. Michèle Roberts – whose novel *Impossible Saints* owes much to Ovid's *Heroines' Letters* – rewrites Hypsipyle's letter to Jason. Roberts' letter unashamedly re-stages Ovid's *Heroines' Letters* 6 in modern dress – just as Ovid recast his ancient Greek heroines as his own Roman contemporaries, directing them to speak and act as Augustan *puellae*. But while some readers will undoubtedly criticise such responses to Ovid, seeing them as 'frothy trivializations', others may see it as remarkable that almost two millennia after his death Ovid has not yet gone out of fashion. As literary historian Theodore Ziolkowski observes:

> From the ancient *tenerorum lusor amorum*, the medieval *Ovidius Christianus* and *Ovide moralisé*, and the *Ovidius redivivus* and *Ovide travesti* of the Renaissance, Ovid has progressed by way of Ovid baroque'd and rococo'd to such recent manifestations as Ovid eroticized, nationalized, psychologized, and trivialized. Every age gets the Ovid it deserves. What sort of Ovid will the new millennium bring forth? Where, indeed, can it go beyond the frothy trivializations at the turn of the millennium?

In his froth-free poem 'Ovid in Tomis', the Northern Irish poet Derek Mahon directs us towards one Ovid for the third millennium. Ovid's exile from Rome is used in Mahon's poem to explore the sense of alienation and personal exile that is seen to characterise life in the postmodern world. Exiled from Rome where his name has long since become 'A dirty word', Mahon's Ovid knows that he can never return to the city – he can never truly go home. Banished from Rome a long time ago to live on the edge of the civilised world, separated from his wife, his daughter, his friends, his home, Mahon reminds us that Ovid was never 'really' a Roman in the first place. But, as an exile from Augustan Rome, Ovid seems peculiarly at home in our postmodern brave new world. Here, we are all exiles. Here, the old gods – pagan and Christian – have been transformed into 'a gear-box in the rain beside the road'. Here, Ovid has metamorphosed into a stone. He knows that he is 'Not poet enough' to write any more. A blank sheet of paper, 'woven of wood-nymphs', becomes the object of his veneration and his last words.

> I incline my head
> To its candour
> And weep for our exile.

Glossary

Achilles Principal Greek hero of the Trojan war and Homer's *Iliad*, lover of Briseis

Aeneas Trojan hero of Homer's *Iliad* and Virgil's *Aeneid*, son of Venus (Aphrodite), and legendary founder of Rome

aetas Ovidiana Latin term: 'age of Ovid' – used by medievalist Ludwig Traube to describe the popularity of Ovid in the twelfth and thirteenth centuries

aetiology A story telling of origins or causes

Agamemnon Principal Greek leader in the Trojan war and Homer's *Iliad*

amor Latin term: 'love' – but also 'sex, a lover, a beloved, the god Love, or Cupid'

Andromache Wife of Trojan hero Hector

Ariadne Daughter of king Minos and Pasiphaë, and lover of Athenian prince Theseus

Aurora Goddess of the Dawn and mother of Memnon

Automedon Achilles' charioteer

Briseis Achilles' slave and lover

Byblis Twin sister of Caunus, with whom she falls in love

Callimachus Greek poet, author of the *Aetia* (*Causes*), and 'emperor of elegy' (*princeps elegiae*) to the Roman love poets

Canace Sister of Macareus, with whom she falls in love

Catullus Roman love poet

Clytemnestra Wife of Greek king Agamemnon and lover of Aegisthus

consul Latin term: title given to the two chief magistrates of Rome

Creusa First wife of Aeneas, abandoned at Troy

Cynthia Elegiac mistress of Propertius

Deidamia Daughter of King Lycomedes of Scyros, raped by Achilles and mother of his son, Neoptolemus (or Pyrrhus)

Demophoön Son of Theseus and Phaedra, lover of Phyllis

didactic Classical genre of poetry, usually written in hexameters, designed to instruct its readers on some art or craft

Dido Legendary Carthaginian queen and lover of Aeneas

domina Latin term: elegiac 'mistress'

ego Latin term: the persona that speaks 'I' in elegy

elegy Classical genre of poetry, comprising one hexameter and one pentameter line. Used for poetry about mythology and warfare, politics and pederasty, love poems, laments, and drinking songs, but originally associated with grave dedications and funeral epitaphs

epic Classical genre of poetry, written in hexameter, concerned with legendary, historic, and martial themes

erotodidactic Sub-genre of didactic poetry designed to instruct readers on erotic technique

ethopoeia Rhetorical exercise of speaking as another character

Euripides Greek tragedian

Europa Phoenician princess, raped by Jupiter, mother of Minos

exclusus amator Latin term: 'a lover shut out', a popular motif in Latin love elegy

exempla Latin term: 'example' or 'paradigm'

exsilium Latin term: 'exile' – a formal punishment

fallax opus Latin term: 'deceitful genre/work' – term used to describe elegy

fasti Latin term: 'calendar' – but also 'legal', 'allowed', and 'speech'

Gallus Early writer of Latin love elegy, and author of the *Loves* (*Amores*) addressed to a mistress he calls Lycoris

Hermione Daughter of Menelaus and Helen, lover of Orestes

hexameter A poetic metre comprising six units or feet, traditionally used for epic verse

Horace Roman poet

Hypsipyle Lemnian princess and lover of Jason

iambic Classical genre of poetry associated with sexually explicit and satirical verse

iocus Latin term: 'joke'

Jason Greek hero, leader of the Argonauts, and lover of Medea and Hypsipyle

kore Greek term: 'girl'

Laodamia Wife of the first Greek to be slain by the Trojans, Protesilaus, who killed herself to be with her husband in Hades

Lara A nymph, raped by the god Mercury, mother of the Roman Lares

lex Julia Latin term: 'Julian laws', legislation passed in 18 BC making adultery a criminal offence

Livia Wife and consort of Augustus

Lotis A nymph whom Priapus tries to rape

Lucretia Wife of Collatinus, raped by Tarquinius Superbus, catalyst for the expulsion of the kings of Rome, and Roman paradigm of feminine honour and chastity

magister amoris Latin term: 'professor of love', and Ovid's alter ego in the *Art of Love*

matrona Latin term: respectable 'married woman' of the Roman aristocracy

Medea Lover of Jason and legendary witch

meretrix Latin term: 'courtesan' – but also 'call-girl' or 'prostitute'

metre The rhyme scheme in which poetry is composed

militia amoris Latin term: 'love as war', a common elegiac trope

mores Latin term: 'customs' – but also 'fashions'

Myrrha Daughter of Cinyras, with whom she falls in love

Oenone Trojan nymph and lover of Paris

Orestes Son of Agamemnon and Clytemnestra, lover of Hermione

Paris Trojan prince and lover of Helen and Oenone

Pasiphaë Wife of Minos who falls in love with a bull and bears the monstrous Minotaur

Penelope Wife of Ulysses (Odysseus), paradigm of wifely virtue and chastity

pentameter A poetic metre comprising five units or feet

Penthesilea Amazon queen and warrior, killed by Achilles

Persephone Daughter of the goddess Demeter (Ceres), raped by Pluto, god of the Underworld

Phaedra Wife of Theseus who falls in love with her stepson, Hippolytus

Phyllis Thracian queen and lover of Demophoön

praeceptor amoris Latin term: 'professor of love' and one of Ovid's alter egos in the *Art of Love*

Priapus An ithyphallic god familiar for his huge, permanently erect penis

princeps Latin term: 'emperor'

Propertius Latin love elegist and predecessor to Ovid

puella Latin term: 'girl' – but also 'sweetheart' or 'darling'

purple stripe A mark of high social status and maturity

recusatio Poetic defence or justification for choice of literary form

reductio ad absurdam Latin term: 'to reduce to the absurd' – satirising or mocking a viewpoint or argument

relegatio Latin term: 'banishment'

Rhea Silvia A vestal virgin, raped by the god Mars, mother of the twins Romulus and Remus

Sappho Greek love poet

servus Latin term: 'slave' and common elegiac figure

servitium amoris Latin term: 'love as slavery', a common elegiac trope

Tibullus Latin love elegist and predecessor to Ovid
Tiphys Helmsman of the Argo
Tomis Location of Ovid's exile
topoi Latin term: 'commonplaces' or 'themes'
trope The figurative or metaphoric use of language
tu mihi sola places Latin term: 'you alone please me'– but also 'you are the one for me' or 'I love you'
Venus Goddess of love, goddess of sex, mother of Cupid or Love, mother of Aeneas and thus mother of the Roman race, founder-mother (*genetrix*) of the Julian line, patron of love poetry
Vesta Goddess of the hearth
uis (vis) Latin term: 'force' – but also 'violence, rape'

Note on Translations

There are countless English translations of Ovid's elegiac works. Some are elegant and entertaining, successfully reproducing the character of the originals, and some are frankly not. The Harvard University Press Loeb Library editions offer English prose translations (by various authors) alongside the Latin texts of each for readers with some Latin. Those who prefer more up-to-date translations that still follow the Latin closely have a wide range of options open to them. Peter Green has produced a fine translation of Ovid's *Amores* (*Loves*), *Ars Amatoria* (*Art of Love*), and *Remedia Amoris* (*Cures for Love*) under the collective title of *Erotic Poems*, and he has also translated the *Tristia* (*Sad Songs*) and *Epistulae ex Ponto* (*Letters from Pontus*) in *The Poems of Exile*. Harold Isbell has translated the *Heroides* (*Heroines' Letters*), while Anthony Boyle and Roger Woodward offer a translation of the *Fasti* (*Calendar*). All of these Penguin translations are commonly used by students, and are also successful in making Ovid's writing accessible to the general reader.

But readers looking for 'poetry' in their translations of Ovid's elegiac works should try versions produced by other poets. Among the earliest and best-known English translations of Ovid's erotic elegy is Christopher Marlowe's *All Ovids Elegies*, first published around 1600. Written in pentameter couplets, Marlowe's translation attempts to reproduce the effect of Ovid's elegiac metre in English and, although its language and its rhyme scheme can seem monotonous after a while, it captures the playfulness and humour of the original well. In comparison, John Dryden's widely read translations of the *Amores* (*Loves*) and *Ars Amatoria* (*Art of Love*) from the 1680s still retain their freshness and accessibility to a modern audience, but can sometimes seem to lack Marlowe's vitality. Among the poets who have tackled Ovid's elegies more recently, Guy Lee has a good translation of the *Amores* (*Loves*) that nicely captures the nuances of the original. Daryl Hine offers an appropriately witty version of the *Heroides* (*Heroines' Letters*) and Derek Mahon, author of *Ovid in Tomis*, has also sensitively translated selections from the *Amores* (*Loves*) into English, while David Slavitt's exquisite translations – or perhaps a better term might be 'transformations' – of Ovid's exile poems have prompted classicists to look at the *Tristia* (*Sad Songs*) and *Epistulae ex Ponto* (*Letters from Pontus*) with new appreciation.

Christopher Martin's excellent *Ovid in English* offers a comprehensive collection of translations and adaptations of Ovid's poetry from Chaucer to classicist Betty Rose Nagle, and is well worth reading. Full details of this work and all other translations cited here can be found in the bibliography.

Further Reading

Our modern *aetas Ovidiana* has seen a wealth of material recently published on Ovid and his elegiac writing, and these suggestions for further reading are necessarily highly selective. Sara Myers offers a useful survey of recent scholarly work on Ovid in her bibliographical essay 'The Metamorphosis of a Poet', and readers may find further ideas for reading and research there. Full details of each work recommended here can be found in the bibliography.

Two recent, scholarly, and broadly comprehensive works on Ovid, *The Cambridge Companion to Ovid* and *Brill's Companion to Ovid*, both contain important essays on individual poems and on general Ovidian themes. These Companions are designed as accessible handbooks for general readers who want to read more about Ovid, and contain some provocative contributions also aimed at academics and students. Sara Mack's *Ovid* and L.P. Wilkinson's *Ovid Recalled* (abridged as *Ovid Surveyed*) both provide good starting points for those looking for a more general overview of the poet and his work.

On the subject of Latin love elegy, Duncan Kennedy's *The Art of Love* is an essential work, developing many of the ideas found in Paul Veyne's *Roman Erotic Elegy* – also invaluable for readers interested in this area. R.O.A.M. Lyne's *The Latin Love Poets* offers a useful and accessible introduction, while Ellen Greene's work on *The Erotics of Domination* demonstrates the value of feminist approaches to Latin love poetry, especially Ovid. For those readers who are not afraid of theory and who might like to learn more about *A Lover's Discourse*, I highly recommend Roland Barthes' work of the same name.

Readers interested in the reception and influence of Ovid's elegiac poetry in later literature should try *Ovid and the Moderns* by Theodore Ziolkowski as the best and most comprehensive work available on Ovid's place in modern literature. Studies of Ovid's influence tend to focus predominately on his epic *Metamorphoses* at the expense of his elegiac writing, but E.K. Rand's *Ovid and his Influence* has some good material on the elegies. Similarly, some of the essays edited by Charles Martindale in his excellent *Ovid Renewed*, and William S. Anderson in *Ovid: The Classical Heritage*, have interesting things to say about the reception of Ovid's erotic and exilic elegies.

Some readers may want to pursue a particular interest in one of Ovid's individual works and there are plenty of articles and volumes available to satisfy that interest. For further recommendations and ideas for suggested reading on specific poems, the more detailed bibliographies included in the books below should help. On the *Loves*, J.C. McKeown's commentaries are excellent, and Barbara Weiden Boyd offers a rare survey of all three books in *Ovid's Literary Loves*. Molly Myerowitz gives a very readable study of the *Art of Love* in *Ovid's Games of Love*, complementing the commentaries on Books 1 and 3 by A.S. Hollis and Roy Gibson. On the *Heroines' Letters*, two very useful volumes which offer detailed readings of each of the poems are *Ovid's Toyshop of the Heart* by Florence Verducci and *Ovid's Heroides* by Howard Jacobson. Geraldine Herbert-Brown's historical study of *Ovid and the Fasti*, and Carole Newlands' *Playing with Time* both give fine treatments of the *Calendar*. And I would highly recommend Betty Rose Nagle on *The Poetics of Exile* and John C. Thibault on *The Mystery of Ovid's Exile* to readers interested in Ovid's exile poetry.

Finally, Ovid has inspired several contemporary works of fiction that some readers might like to try. David Malouf's *Imaginary Life*, Christoph Ransmayr's *The Last World*, and David Wishart's *Ovid* draw inspiration from Ovid's exile, while Mavis Cheek's *Aunt Margaret's Lover* and Jane Alison's *The Love-Artist* both draw extensively from Ovid's love poetry.

Bibliography

Alison, Jane, *The Love-Artist* (New York: Farrar, Strauss and Giroux 2001).

Anderson, William. S., ed., *Ovid: The Classical Heritage* (New York: Garland 1995).

Barsby, John, *Ovid: Amores Book I* (Bristol: Bristol Classical Press 1979).

Barthes, Roland, *A Lover's Discourse: Fragments*, translated by Richard Howard (Harmondsworth: Penguin 1990).

Binns, J.W., ed., *Ovid* (London and Boston: Routledge and Kegan Paul 1973).

Boyd, Barbara Weiden, *Ovid's Literary Loves: Influence and Innovation in the Amores* (Ann Arbor: University of Michigan Press 1997).

Boyd, Barbara Weiden, ed., *Brill's Companion to Ovid* (Leiden: Brill 2002).

Boyle, A.J., and Woodward, R.D., *Fasti* (Harmondsworth: Penguin 2000).

Braund, S.M. and Mayer, R., eds, *Amor: Roma. Love and Latin Literature* (Cambridge: Cambridge University Press 1999).

Cahoon, Leslie, 'The Bed as Battlefield: Erotic Conquest and Military Metaphor in Ovid's *Amores*', in *Transactions of the American Philological Association* 118 (1988), pp. 293-307.

Cheek, Mavis, *Aunt Margaret's Lover* (London: Hamish Hamilton 1994).

Davis, J.T., *Fictus Adulter: Poet as Actor in the Amores* (Amsterdam: Gieben 1989).

Dryden, John, *The Poems of John Dryden*, edited by James Kinsley (Oxford: Clarendon Press 1958).

Edwards, C., *The Politics of Immorality in Ancient Rome* (Cambridge: Cambridge University Press 1993).

Eggers, Dave, Krauss, Nicole, the Staff of McSweeney's, and Safron Foer, Jonathan, *The Future Dictionary of America* (London: Hamish Hamilton 2004).

Evans, Harry, *Publica Carmina: Ovid's Books from Exile* (Lincoln: University of Nebraska Press 1983).

Fantham, Elaine, 'Sexual Comedy in Ovid's *Fasti*: Sources and Motivations', in *Harvard Studies in Classical Philology* 87 (1983), pp. 185-216.

Farrell, Joe, 'Reading and Writing the *Heroides*', in *Harvard Studies in Classical Philology* 98 (1998), pp. 307-38.

Feeney, D.C., '*Si licet et fas est*: Ovid's *Fasti* and the Problem of Free Speech Under the Principate', in *Roman Poetry and Propaganda in the Age of Augustus*, edited by A. Powell (Bristol: Bristol Classical Press 1992), pp. 1-25.

Frazer, J.G., *The Golden Bough: A History of Myth and Religion* (London: Chancellor Press 1994).

Frazer, J.G., *Ovid: Fasti* (Cambridge, MA and London: Harvard University Press 1996).

Gibson, Roy, *A Commentary on Ovid Ars Amatoria III* (Cambridge: Cambridge University Press 2003).

Graves, Robert, *Poems (1914-1926)* (London: Heinemann 1927).

Green, Peter, *Ovid: The Erotic Poems* (Harmondsworth: Penguin 1982).

Green, Peter, *Ovid: The Poems of Exile* (Harmondsworth: Penguin 1994).

Greene, E. *The Erotics of Domination: Male Desire and the Mistress in Latin Love Elegy* (Baltimore: Johns Hopkins University Press 1998).

Habinek, Tom, *The Politics of Latin Literature: Writing, Identity, and Empire in Ancient Rome* (Princeton: Princeton University Press 1998).

Hallett, J.P. and Skinner, M.B., eds, *Roman Sexualities* (Princeton: Princeton University Press 1997).

Hardie, Philip, ed., *The Cambridge Companion to Ovid* (Cambridge: Cambridge University Press 2002).

Harrison, Stephen, 'Ovid and Genre: The Evolutions of an Elegist', in Hardie (2002), pp. 79-94.

Herbert-Brown, Geraldine, *Ovid and the Fasti: An Historical Study* (Oxford: Clarendon Press 1994).

Hinds, Stephen, 'Booking the Return Trip: Ovid and *Tristia* 1', in *Proceedings of the Cambridge Philological Society* 31(1985), pp. 13-32.

Hine, Daryl, *Ovid's Heroines: A Verse Translation of the Heroides* (New Haven: Yale University Press 1991).

Hollis, A.S., *Ovid Ars Amatoria Book 1* (Oxford: Oxford University Press 1977).

Isbell, Harold, *Heroides* (Harmondsworth: Penguin 1990).

Kennedy, Duncan, *The Arts of Love: Five Studies in the Discourse of Roman Love Elegy* (Cambridge: Cambridge University Press 1993).

Kennedy, Duncan, 'The Epistolary Mode and the First of Ovid's *Heroides*', in *Classical Quarterly* 34 (1984), pp. 413-22.

Kubrick, Stanley and Raphael, Frederic, *Eyes Wide Shut. A Screenplay* (New York: Warner Books 1999).

Jacobson, Howard, *Ovid's Heroides* (Princeton: Princeton University Press 1974).

Kaufmann, L.S., *Discourses of Desire: Gender, Genre, and Epistolary Fictions* (Ithaca and London: Cornell University Press 1986).

Knox, Peter, *Ovid Heroides* (Cambridge: Cambridge University Press 1995).

Lee, A. Guy, *Ovid's Amores* (New York: Viking 1968).

Lyne, R.O.A.M., *The Latin Love Poets from Catullus to Horace* (Oxford: Oxford University Press 1980).

Mack, Sara, *Ovid* (New Haven: Yale University Press 1988).

Mahon, Derek, 'Ovid in Tomis', in *The Hunt by Night* (Winston Salem: Wake Forest University Press 1995), pp. 389-90.

Mahon, Derek, *Selected Poems* (London: Viking 1991).

Malouf, David, *An Imaginary Life* (New York: Braziller 1978).

Marlowe, Christopher, *The Complete Works of Christopher Marlowe*, edited by Roma Gill (Oxford: Clarendon Press 1987).

Martin, Christopher, ed., *Ovid in English* (London: Penguin 1998).

Martindale, Charles, ed., *Ovid Renewed: Ovidian Influences on Literature and Art from the Middle Ages to the Twentieth Century* (Cambridge: Cambridge University Press 1988).

McKeown, J.C., *Ovid Amores I: A Commentary on Book One* (Leeds: Francis Cairns Publications 1989).

McKeown, J.C., *Ovid Amores III: A Commentary on Book Two* (Leeds: Francis Cairns Publications 1998).

Mozeley, J.H., *Ovid: The Art of Love and Other Poems* (Cambridge, MA and London: Harvard University Press 1999).

Myerowitz, Molly, *Ovid's Games of Love* (Detroit: Wayne State University Press 1985).

Myers, S., 'The Metamorphosis of a Poet: Recent Work on Ovid', in *Journal of Roman Studies* 89 (1999), pp. 190-204.

Nagle, Betty Rose, *The Poetics of Exile: Program and Polemic in the Tristia and Epistulae ex Ponto of Ovid* (Brussels: Collection Latomus 170, 1980).

Newlands, Carole, *Playing with Time: Ovid and the Fasti* (Ithaca and London: Cornell University Press 1995).

O'Gorman, Ellen, 'Love and the Family; Augustus and Ovidian Elegy', in *Arethusa* 30.1 (1997), pp. 103-24.

Rand, E.K., *Ovid and His Influence* (New York: Cooper Square Publishers 1963).

Ransmayr, Christoph, *The Last World: With an Ovidian Repertory*, translated by John Woods (New York: Grove Weidenfeld 1990).

Richlin, Amy, ed., *Pornography and Representation in Greece and Rome* (New York and Oxford: Oxford University Press 1992).

Roberts, Michèle, 'Hypsipyle to Jason', in *Ovid Metamorphosed*, edited by Philip Terry (London: Vintage 2000), pp. 53-6.

Rosenmeyer, Patricia, 'Ovid's *Heroides* and *Tristia*: Voices from Exile', in *Ramus* 26.1 (1997), pp. 29-56.

Sharrock, A., 'Womanufacture', in *Journal of Roman Studies* 81 (1991), pp. 36-49.

Showerman, Grant, *Ovid: Heroides and Amores* (Cambridge, MA and London: Harvard University Press 1986).

Slavitt, David, *Ovid's Poetry of Exile* (Baltimore and London: Johns Hopkins University Press 1990).

Spentzou, E., *Reading Characters Read; Transgressions of Gender and Genre in Ovid's Heroides* (Oxford: Oxford University Press 2003).

Stapleton, M.L., *Harmful Eloquence: Ovid's Amores from Antiquity to Shakespeare* (Ann Arbor: University of Michigan Press 1996).

Stoppard, Tom, *Rosencrantz and Guildenstern are Dead* (London: Faber and Faber 1973).

Terry, Philip, ed., *Ovid Metamorphosed* (London: Vintage 2000).

Terry, Philip, 'Void', in Terry (2000), pp. 34-52.

Thibault, J.C., *The Mystery of Ovid's Exile* (Berkeley and Los Angeles: University of Califorina Press 1964).

Verducci, Florence, *Ovid's Toyshop of the Heart: Epistulae Heroidum* (Princeton: Princeton University Press 1985).

Veyne, Paul, *Roman Erotic Elegy: Love, Poetry, and the West*, translated by David Pellauer (Chicago: University of Chicago Press 1988).

West, David, 'Nightfall on the Romanian Coast', in Terry (2000), pp. 219-29.

Wheeler, A.L., *Ovid: Tristia and Ex Ponto* (Cambridge, MA and London: Harvard University Press 1996).

Wilkinson, L.P., *Ovid Recalled* (Cambridge: Cambridge University Press 1955).

Williams, Gareth, *Banished Voices: Readings in Ovid's Exile Poetry* (Cambridge: Cambridge University Press 1994).

Williams, Gareth, 'Writing in the Mother-Tongue: Hermione and Helen in *Heroides* 8 (A Tomitian Approach)', in *Ramus* 26 (1997), pp. 113-37.

Wishart, David, *Ovid* (London: Sceptre 1995).

Wyke, Maria, 'Mistress and Metaphor in Augustan Elegy', in *Helios* 16 (1989), pp.25-47.

Ziolkowski, Theodore, *Ovid and the Moderns* (Ithaca and London: Cornell University Press 2005).

Acknowledgements

The author and publisher are grateful for permission to reproduce copyright material from the following works:

Lines from 'Ovid in Tomis' from *Collected Poems* by Derek Mahon (1999). Used by kind permission of the author and The Gallery Press, Loughcrew, Oldcastle, County Meath, Ireland.
Excerpts from 'Void' by Philip Terry (2000) in *Ovid Metamorphosed* by Philip Terry. Used by kind permission of the author.
Excerpt from 'Ovid in Defeat' from *Poems (1914-1926)* by Robert Graves (Heinemann, 1928). Used by permission of Carcanet Press Ltd.
Extract from 'Nightfall on the Romanian Coast' by Paul West (2000) in *Ovid Metamorphosed* by Philip Terry. Used by kind permission of the author.
Excerpt from 'The Art of Love' by Peter Jones (1989). Used by kind permission of the author.

Every effort has been made to trace all copyright holders, but if any have been overlooked, the author will be pleased to make the necessary arrangements at the first opportunity.

All translations, unless otherwise identified, are the author's.

The author is grateful to Carl Dolan, Duncan Kennedy, Charles Martindale, and Vanda Zajko for their insightful comments – and to the series editor, Deborah Blake, for her patience.

Index